LF

D0592204

© Basil Blackwell Publisher Limited 1984

First published 1984
Basil Blackwell Publisher Limited
108 Cowley Road, Oxford OX4 1JF, England

All rights reserved. Except for the quotation of
short passages for the purposes of criticism and
review, no part of this publication may be reproduced,
stored in a retrieval system, or transmitted, in any
form or by any means, electronic, mechanical, photocopying,
recording or otherwise, without the prior permission of
the publisher.

Except in the United States of America, this book
is sold subject to the condition that it shall not,
by way of trade or otherwise, be lent, re-sold, hired
out, or otherwise circulated without the publisher's
prior consent in any form of binding or cover other than
that in which it is published and without a similar
condition including this condition being imposed on
the subsequent purchaser.

British Library Cataloguing in Publication Data

Leftwich, Adrian
    What is politics?
    1. Politics
    I. Title
    320   JA66

ISBN 0-631-13486-7
ISBN 0-631-13553-7 Pbk

Typesetting by Getset (BTS) Ltd, Eynsham, Oxford
Printed in Great Britain by Camelot Press Ltd, Southampton

ALBRIGHT COLLEGE LIBRARY

320
W 555

194160

Contents

Acknowledgements

The major acknowledgement which an editor of a volume such as this needs to make is to the contributors. All of them responded with enthusiasm to the idea and produced their chapters well within the deadline. In particular, thanks must go to Andrew Dunsire who had to complete his piece in the course of a move from York to Singapore, where he was teaching in the academic year 1983/4.

I should also like to thank Dr Keith Hartley, Director of the Institute for Research in the Social Sciences (IRISS) at the University of York, for agreeing to provide invaluable secretarial support, and to Barbara Dodds of IRISS for organizing it so effectively. In addition, I am grateful to Gale Hadfield who assisted with some of the typing and who helped to prepare the manuscript for the publisher. This made my task much easier when time was short.

Adrian Leftwich

Introduction

On the politics of Politics

ADRIAN LEFTWICH

1

What is politics? To what activities in the world does the term 'politics' refer? Are these found in all societies, past and present, or only some? If only some, then what is distinctive about them and the activities in them which we call politics? Is politics, moreover, found at all levels in such societies, that is in all groups and institutions within them? Or is it only found in some spheres, for instance those concerned with 'government' or the legitimate exercise of force? That is to say, is politics only found in the 'public' sphere and not the 'private'? And, if so, how do we really distinguish between the two and where is the line drawn?

On the other hand, could it not be argued that politics is found in *all* societies, past and present, and that it is a characteristic and necessary feature, or process, wherever the human species is or has been found? If such a view is adopted, then does it not become necessary to abandon the conventional distinction between the 'private' and 'public' worlds and hence be able to identify and analyse politics in and between *all* groups and institutions in all societies, and in the relations between them: for instance, in families, clubs, colleges, companies, states, international organizations and multinational corporations?

These are some of the questions which are addressed in different ways in the following chapters. But a further set of questions follows from these, and they are also considered. How do distinctive definitions and conceptions of politics influence what is or should be taught in the discipline of Politics? In other words, what should be the appropriate focus, content, scope and methods of the academic study called Politics?

The major objective of this book is to introduce readers coming to the serious study of Politics for the first time to some of the many views on these questions, and hence help them to situate their own studies, courses and thinking on these questions in the context of the views outlined here. With a primarily undergraduate readership in mind, all the authors have organized their contributions around the above questions. Throughout, the use of the word 'politics' refers to the activity in the world, and the word 'Politics' to the academic discipline.

A second objective of the book is to stimulate debate among students, and also teachers, about the questions raised here. For there can be nothing more important for any discipline than constant and far-reaching appraisal of, and argument about, its fundamental concerns and approaches.

It is not the purpose of this Introduction to summarize in advance the main lines of interpretation which are offered in the subsequent chapters.[1] Rather, it may be more useful to raise some wider issues concerning the nature of the debate about the definition of politics, and the implications of this for the discipline of Politics. These issues may be worth bearing in mind when reading what follows. Before doing that, however, it may be of interest to readers to know in outline the circumstances under which this volume came about.

2

During the course of 1981, some members of the department of Politics in the University of York became restless about the then current structure of the Honours degree in Politics which had been in operation for almost ten years. They felt that there was a need to devise a more flexible curriculum which offered rather more choice to students. Some of them — a small minority — felt that there was a need for the department to use the occasion of restructuring to rethink entirely the content and method of its teaching and assessment arrangements. They believed this for good intellectual and pedagogic reasons. They also felt that there was a need for the discipline to respond more directly in analytical and teaching terms to at least some of the problems occurring within British and global society, and also in the light of some of the pressures

[1] I am very grateful to Peter Nicholson, Albert Weale and especially David Held for extremely helpful comments on a draft of this introduction, although I alone am responsible for it.

being brought to bear on higher education in general and the social sciences in particular.

During both formal and informal discussions about these issues we all began to learn some very interesting things about each others' views on fundamental questions about politics and its study which we had not known before. To our collective surprise, we realized that, as a department, we had never (at least not since 1970) sat down together to explore these central questions about the activity of politics and the discipline of Politics. Perhaps the most interesting thing we learned was just how far apart – or so it seemed at the time – were the views of members of the department about the major question with which this book is concerned: what is politics? Few of us have any reason to believe that this is untypical of academics in other departments of Politics in Britain and elsewhere.

Our discussions raised many fascinating and difficult issues of theory and practice in relation to teaching, learning, assessing and organizing the discipline of Politics. And, if our experience is anything to go by, *any* group of academics and students will gain an enormous amount by undertaking such an exercise themselves in their own department or faculty. To ask fundamental questions of this kind is to confront one's own and others' often dated assumptions, preferences, priorities, commitments and habits of mind and practice. To have to advance and defend one's views in the context of trying to produce a coherent set of proposals for a degree in Politics is a very salutary exercise, not least because it compels one to ask – rather more openly than most of us like to do – questions such as: What are our intellectual and pedagogic objectives? Are we achieving them? If not, why not? Is this or that what a degree in Politics in the last twenty years of the twentieth century should be about?

The outcome of these discussions about course reorganization is not necessary to record here, although satisfaction with the new structure was neither universal nor equal in terms of enthusiasm. This point may illustrate some of the interesting arguments which Albert Weale develops in his chapter about politics as collective choice, and some of the unpredictable (and unwanted) consequences which may sometimes flow from it.

Be that as it may, it seemed a good idea to make some of the differences in approach to politics and Politics which emerged in this exercise more widely available, since there are currently no books on the market which do so in this fashion. This book is the outcome of that idea.

Most of the authors participated actively in the discussions about course revision.[2] While they have not had a chance to see each other's final drafts, all have read the main lines of the arguments in summary form, as some of the cross-references in the various chapters indicate.

The present volume is offered in the hope that it will help to stimulate further thinking, argument and writing on the main questions, and hence help to strengthen the discipline of Politics and improve our understanding of politics. As Peter Nicholson argues in his chapter, no student of Politics can avoid making his or her choice of a definition of politics, and it is important to face this issue early in one's studies and to continue thinking about it. In doing just that, readers may be able to criticize, develop, integrate or abandon the offerings presented here, or to evolve their own.

Against this background, what implications and issues of a more general kind arise from the questions addressed here? I think there are several important ones concerning the politics of Politics which are important to raise at the start of such a book.

3

The first point concerns the very nature of an academic discipline. The term 'discipline' means, simply, a field of study. It is important for those coming fresh to the study of Politics (or any other discipline for that matter) to realize that it is *not* a God-given, officially defined or authoritative demarcation. Nor is it a hard and fast area of study whose character and scope we have to take for granted, or assume to be unchanging or permanent for all time. Disciplines, that is to say, have not arrived fully formed in the world of science. Like all other aspects of social life, they evolve and change over time in the course of their interaction with their environment, with each other, and in response to problems occurring within them and between them and their ultimate point of reference, the 'real' world.

In general, disciplines are distinguished from each other by the typical kinds of problems with which they concern themselves; by the typical

---

[2] Midway through the discussions we lost David Held to the Open University, but he helped to formulate ideas which were later incorporated into the revised course structure.

kinds of questions which they ask about such problems; and by the kinds of theoretical and analytical frameworks in terms of which they both ask the questions and attempt to answer them. Disciplines, that is to say, are defined by an intimate combination of their theoretical and conceptual frameworks, and their empirical and problematic referents. So, too, are distinctive 'schools' within them.

Perhaps more important still, for present purposes, disciplines are constituted largely by conventions, and they are sustained by communities of scholars who work within them. That is to say, the characteristic features, boundaries and procedures of disciplines are fashioned by human beings, sustained by them and changed by them. Given that this is the case, it is crucial for the vitality of any discipline that succeeding generations of students and teachers in them do not accept passively the prevailing definitions and conventions which they encounter when they come to study them or teach them. A respect (and sometimes reverence) for authority is a common feature of social life in all societies, and those to whom it is given usually seek to sustain it. Whether that is a good thing or not is another question. But if it leads to uncritical acceptance of prevailing ways of doing things, or thinking about them, it can only lead to stagnation. And since change, in my view, is the very essence of growth and life, a discipline which does not encourage its students to question, redefine and reorganize its assumptions, substantive concerns and theoretical frameworks can only wither. If a discipline does not constantly question the nature and methods of its engagement with and analysis of the problems of the world – contemporary or historical – it will, like some aspects of medieval scholarship, lose contact with the central issues of secular life and become irrelevant to both people and their concerns. This is nowhere more true than for the social sciences. So there are, in principle, good reasons for raising fundamental questions of this kind about the discipline of Politics, and for stimulating debate about what we do, how we do it and why.

4

Secondly, I think it can be argued, although some of the contributors to this volume would be opposed to this view (given their conceptions of politics), that the very debate over the definition of politics and the proper structure and scope of the discipline of Politics is itself, in crucial respects, a political debate with profoundly political implications, though it is not only that. I think this can be illustrated briefly at several levels, in micro, meso and macro terms.

The micro sense is best illustrated with reference to the chapters of this book. For the way in which the subject matter of politics is defined, locally in a department, has a strong influence on how the discipline will be constituted and studied locally. That is to say, the definition and delimitation of the subject-matter of politics will shape what is taught and, in some respects, how it is taught. By this I do *not* mean that *one* conception of politics will produce one particular interpretation of political life (be it Conservative, Liberal or Socialist, in British party terms, for instance), which will then be pushed at students. For there will always be more or less clear differences in approach and interpretation, whatever the breadth or narrowness of a particular conception of politics. For example, a Conservative and a Socialist might agree in general that politics is about the struggle for power and authority at the level of the state (and between states), but they would have very different ways of analysing such struggles and very different interpretations of, and judgements about, their causes, conditions and consequences. A concern with the state, furthermore, is one shared by functionalists, systems-analysts and Marxists. So a given conception of what politics is about does *not* lead to identical interpretations or judgements about it in any given instance.

What I *do* mean, however, is that the conception or conceptions of politics which predominate in a particular department will, for instance, influence the kinds of specialist staff that are sought and appointed (and hence professorial power can be significant in this respect), and in due course will come to influence the composition and balance of the department, and hence what is taught. If, for example, the predominant view in a department is that the proper and central focus of the discipline is the comparative study of government, it is unlikely that many teachers (if any) will be appointed who have done field-work in local-level politics amongst, say, the Tallensi of Northern Ghana, or the inhabitants of a shanty town around Sao Paulo, in Brazil. In these and other ways the local 'academic culture' of a department develops, and this has a major influence over the years on what is taught, by whom and in what ways. [3] And, as is the case with all forms of culture, these

[3] I have discussed the question of a departmental 'academic culture' elsewhere. See chapter 4 of the present volume, and Adrian Leftwich, *Redefining Politics: People, Resources and Power* (London, 1983), ch. 5.

established ways of doing things seldom change quickly.

Thus the composition and culture of a department – which *both* reflect and influence its politics – will, at most, determine what questions, issues and problems are included *in* the syllabus, and – as Sam Goldwyn is alleged to have said in very different circumstances – included *out*.[4] And, at least, the predominating conceptions will fashion the context and structure within which non-predominant conceptions are presented and, hence, either marginalize or distort them.

The political nature and implications of the debate over the definition of politics and the proper scope of research in Politics can be illustrated in middle-level (or meso) terms with reference, for instance, to the kinds of research priorities that are supported and funded. It is, for example, unlikely that a significant amount of official (say, Britain's Social Science Research Council) funding would find its way in the direction of a series of major research projects (in political theory or philosophy, for instance) concerned with the exploration and clarification of conceptual issues and terms in political argument. It is equally improbable that there would be ample funds available from the SSRC for a large-scale comparative analysis of the failure of revolutionary change in modern industrial societies and the appropriate means and strategies for advancing revolutionary movements designed to overthrow the state, although this could certainly be thought of as 'applied' research in Politics of a very fundamental kind. Even a casual glance at information about 'New SSRC Grants', which is published regularly in the *SSRC Newsletter*, will show that the major bulk of grants is devoted to more or less interesting institutional issues to do with local or national governments and their machinery.[5]

Of course this can in part be explained with reference to some of the points discussed above about the micropolitics of Politics: that is, the kind and interests of personnel in Politics departments, who they are and how they got there. It can also be in part explained in comparable terms by looking at the members of the relevant SSRC committees responsible for allocating funds, and determining how they got there. Now it would be a sign of a fraught and highly conspiratorial mind for anyone to believe that research in social science (and Politics in particular, but the same certainly applies to Economics) is directed and dictated, in Britain at least, by the government – through, say, the Department of Education and Science via the SSRC But only the innocence of a fairy

---

[4] Stephen Lukes makes a similar point about the kinds of issues which are and are not allowed to be raised politically, in his *Power: A Radical View* (London, 1974).

[5] See the *SSRC Newsletter* (London, at regular intervals).

would lead one to believe that those responsible for allocating funds for research are not fully (and perhaps anxiously) aware of what would no doubt be called 'official thinking' on research priorities.

As a matter of fact, the formal disciplinary categories of 'Politics' and 'Political Science' have simply vanished from the conceptual map of the social sciences as reflected in the recently reorganized committee structure of the SSRC. So, too, for the record, have International Relations, Sociology and Anthropology. It would seem that 'Politics' and 'Political Science' has been swallowed up in a new committee called 'Government and Law', while some of the substantive concerns of sociologists and anthropologists have been dismembered and their care and encouragement distributed to such new committees as 'Social Affairs', 'Education and Human Development' and 'Environment and Planning'.[6]

It would also appear that the priority research areas which the 'Government and Law' committee of the SSRC hopes to encourage and support are: the monitoring of legislation, regulatory activities of government bodies, and administrative discretion (the 'Law' part of the committee will be hoping to support work on criminological research, justice, family and socio-legal studies).[7] In an initial statement on the general focus of the 'Government and Law' committee, the SSRC stated:

> This will be concerned with the State's decision making institutions, the processes by which decisions are arrived at and the implementation and outcome of policy decisions; with the formation and activities of the political groups involved in these activities. It will also be concerned with the relationship between the State and the individual, and the political organization of economic and social activity. The committee will also cover the political ordering of relationships between states which include a concern with the strategic or defence policies and dispositions of states.[8]

No one would question the importance of such matters, if one could be sure of what some of them really are. But it does seem that, in the

[6] Social Science Research Council (SSRC), *A Change in Structure for Changing Circumstances* (London, 1981).
[7] *Times Higher Education Supplement*, 15 July 1983.
[8] SSRC, *A Change in Structure*.

face of a contracting budget, in the context of government criticism and in the light of the later anxiety associated with the Rothschild enquiry into its activities, the SSRC has played safe in the reorganization of its structure and focus – especially as regards Politics, but not only that. [9]

It is also clear that the conception of politics which underpins its organizational arrangements, committee purview and research priorities is one which is almost obsessively wedded to the role and activities of government. It seems that the SSRC has opted for the politically safer sphere of managerial, administrative and organizational research of a kind which accepts the current institutional and political arrangements, and which acts more or less as a handmaiden to government needs (on a 'customer-contract' basis), rather than opting for what might be termed 'deep structure' research. In short, it is improbable that fundamental research of a theoretical and empirical kind into the structure, viability and relations of economy, society and state – at all levels – will emerge in the next decade under SSRC auspices.

Interesting work will no doubt flow from SSRC-supported research, although we shall have to wait and see. But it seems likely that the influence of this (in terms of funding and personnel, for example) will in turn be reflected in time more generally in the composition and shape of the discipline of Politics (or will we now have to say 'Government'?).

So the micro and meso politics of these matters which concern the definition of politics, research in politics and its implications for the discipline of Politics are not unrelated – although, of course, there are other influences and sources of funds, but not many and not much: nor do they have the financial resources of such official agencies as the SSRC, and the number of SSRC-funded graduate students in Politics is shrinking (which is also true for the social sciences as a whole).

But the political nature of the debate about the definition of politics can also be illustrated with respect to yet broader national, or macro, considerations. It is probably true to say in this respect that in general the more conservative (by which I mean pursuing a strategy which is supportive of 'authority' and defensive of a *status quo* or a *status quo ante*, and *not* a particular political party) a government is, the narrower its view of politics is likely to be, and the less inclined it will be to encourage political debate, research and participation in relation to a wide

[9] Lord Rothschild, *An Enquiry into the Social Science Research Council*, Cmnd. 8554 (London, 1982).

range of social, economic and administrative matters.[10] In short, conservative regimes in this sense – *not* in the simple party political sense – almost always attempt to 'take issues out' of politics; to confine them to executive, administrative or managerial domains and – crucially – to reduce the scope for popular involvement and the raising of awkward issues. Such regimes are also typically much more secretive about their procedures, and much more closed to public scrutiny. For the fact of the matter is that the wider the scope for effective participation in decision-making (that is, the more even the distribution of power), and the more access a public has to information, the less concentration of power there can be at the top – and this is true for state and society as a whole as well as for institutions and organizations within them.

I make these points primarily to stress the earlier line of argument that the debate about the definition of politics is political in both character and implication. Students in the discipline of Politics need to recognize this. For, in varying degrees, in different societies and at different times, the micro, meso and macro politics and implications of the debate about 'what is politics' are connected. They thus have important consequences for what people study, research and – more generally – participate in.

5

I think it is fair to say that the single most important factor involved in influencing the way people implicitly or explicitly conceive of politics is whether they define it primarily in terms of a *process*, or whether they define it in terms of the place or places where it happens, that is in terms of an *arena*, or institutional forum.[11] Those who tend to regard politics as being confined to certain activities within a certain kind of forum (the state, the institutions of government, etc.) will be less inclined to accept that politics is a much more generalized process in human societies. On the other hand, those who see it as a process will be more inclined to

[10]   For one conservative, at least, conservatism is 'dedicated to maintaining the structure and institutions of a society threatened by mercantile enthusiasm and social unrest'; and conservatism is 'the sense of the continuity and vitality of an existing social order'. These quotations are drawn from Roger Scruton, *The Meaning of Conservatism* (Harmondsworth, 1980), pp. 15 and 18, but see chs 1, 2 and 3 especially.

[11]   My thanks to Albert Weale for discussions which helped to clarify this point.

identify it in a far wider range of groups, institutions and societies than the former group. Of course, there is an overlap between the two approaches: for example, many writers on politics in the second category (the arena approach) do sometimes regard it as a process, but confine the processes of politics to certain kinds of institutions and organizations. Likewise, those who see politics as a process may be inclined to confine it to a more or less wide range of institutions, and exclude others. But for most people, the definition of what politics is will fall at a point formed where the dimensions of process and arena intersect for them.

Even then, similar definitions of politics neither automatically flow from nor lead to similar ways of analysing it; nor do they lead to or from similar ideologies or preferences about it. But having said that, I think it may generally be found to be the case that the less ambiguous and the more clear-cut the definition of politics an individual holds, the more likely is he or she to have a preferential mode for its analysis. I think this point is borne out in the chapters by Graeme Moodie, Albert Weale, Alex Callinicos and myself – although there are important differences in approach and method.

6

It may be useful and interesting to reflect a bit on *why* people have such different views on this subject. Clearly, without a most detailed analysis of an individual's history, personality and outlook, it is impossible to do anything else than raise some questions and make some suggestions for further self-reflection and enquiry.

I have already suggested that the more conservative a government is (that is, the more committed it is to the support of 'authority' and defence of the *status quo*), the more inclined it will be to limit the conception and practice of politics. By implication, the opposite is true. The more radical, democratic, open and innovatory a regime is (that is, the more it is committed both to change *and* popular participation), the wider will be its conception of politics and its encouragement of it – although there are seldom many such regimes in the world for very long. Could the same be true for us as individuals? Do the views represented in this volume – and elsewhere more widely in Politics departments up and down the country – correlate more or less closely with broader political outlooks in the conventional sense of the term?

If, as I have suggested, the debate about the definition of politics is political in its character and implications, then our own political views may influence our conceptions of politics. And yet this suggestion is not altogether easy to sustain. For while Graeme Moodie, John Horton and Alex Callinicos converge in some respects in their primary identification of politics with activities concerned with the state and state power, their political outlooks (in the conventional sense) are different in a number of significant respects. Likewise, while Albert Weale, David Held and myself have a more processual view of politics, we are far from unanimous in political outlook.

Secondly, considerations other than these somewhat diffuse political ones may directly influence the way people define and conceive of politics and the appropriate methods for its study. One such consideration – as Graeme Moodie, John Horton and Peter Nicholson all suggest in their chapters in different ways – is that of straightforward manageability. They might be inclined to argue that if the conception of politics is as wide, for instance, as that which David Held and I suggest, then the subject-matter loses any clear focus, and the discipline of Politics becomes substantively and methodologically undisciplined, merging with everything else and floating upwards and downwards, now here, now there, between different levels, and expanding and contracting in scope between micro and macro politics, small informal groupings (such as the family) and large formal institutions of the state and transnational corporations. But flexibility in focus, level and scope – as Andrew Dunsire suggests in his chapter – is not in itself a symptom of lack of discipline. He argues that a broad conception of politics may be rendered manageable in practice by applying a well-organized framework of levels, which he outlines and illustrates.

Third, one might also ask whether the diverse conceptions of politics found in the following chapters may not have something to do with a mixture of interest, temperament and academic background in the case of the individuals concerned. This is of course a very difficult area to analyse, but some points are worth considering since they may throw some light on similar differences which may be found elsewhere. It is often, but not always, the case that the broader conceptions of politics are held by those who have come to research and teaching in the discipline of Politics by way of other disciplines – such as History, Anthropology, Sociology and Economics, or even Theology and English – or may have been strongly influenced in their approach by work in such fields, or some combination of them. The generally wider and more comparative commitments and areas of enquiry of such disciplines – and the influence of significant scholars in them – may merge with or stimulate intellectual interests and temperaments which find it difficult to remain confined to what may seem highly specialized or tight disciplinary compartments, or manageable fields of study. People with such backgrounds may have discovered in their initial studies that such disciplines provide interesting and important insights into the politics of human communities but are, in themselves, limited by their own disciplinary restrictions. And they may come to Politics in the belief and hope that it can provide the context within which broader interdisciplinary explanatory accounts may be more effectively developed.

The opposite route to a broad interdisciplinary view of politics may also occur. For instance, a young graduate student going out to look at political conflict in a particular society (say, Ulster or Cyprus or Zimbabwe or Sri Lanka) may discover rather quickly that it cannot be understood within the typical explanatory categories of Politics (or Political Science or Government), but requires a much wider and fuller understanding of the distribution of, for instance, economic power and the social structure of the society concerned. Such experience may lead him or her to realize the limitations of a narrow view of politics, and to begin to expand his or her definitional (and hence analytical) perspectives. The same is of course true in other areas of research – both within and outside the social sciences. For instance, in recent years people working in the medical sphere have come to recognize how important are social, political and economic factors in the epidemiology of such problems as heart disease, cancers, bronchitis, alcoholism and of course all the killer diseases of the nineteenth century in early industrial Britain.

In short, those with broad conceptions of politics may have come to hold such views because their experience has taught them that narrow disciplinary perspectives are least able to cope analytically with a great variety of problems which occur in human societies. They may agree with the anthropologist, Marvin Harris, who writes that his excuse 'for venturing across disciplines, continents and centuries is that the world extends across disciplines, continents and centuries. Nothing in nature is quite so separate as two mounds of expertise.' [12] To paraphrase this,

[12] Marvin Harris, *Cows, Pigs, Wars and Witches* (Glasgow, 1977), p. 8.

their training, background or experience may have led those with a wide conception of politics to hold such a view because they feel that nothing in the 'real' world corresponds to the sharp distinctions between the conventional focal concerns of disciplines, especially within the social sciences. For them specialization may mean fragmentation.

It would be incorrect to suggest that those with a narrow view of politics are more interested in detailed or empirically rigorous studies than those with a broader view. It would be equally wrong to suggest that the latter are more likely to be concerned with theoretical questions, for all forms of enquiry and study inescapably involve the use of theory. But it is the case that those with a narrower conception of politics are usually interested in a fairly limited class of problems and issues; they may be more inclined towards description, clarification and reflection. On the other hand, those with wide conceptions of politics are usually more interested in explanation and the generation of hypotheses in the context of broad, comparative and holistic studies. They may be more at home in looking for connections, relations and general patterns in social wholes, especially with reference to the structure and characteristics of particular societies and comparatively between them. In yet other words, those with broader conceptions of politics may regard themselves as being more centrally in the tradition of social science with the study of Politics as its integrating focus, whereas those with a narrower view may really be interested in the study of government.

7

It is important to stress that the selection of conceptions – broad and narrow – contained in the chapters which follow does *not* by any manner of means exhaust *all* the views about politics or Politics, at York or anywhere else, although they do represent the main contributions to the discussions at York which were referred to earlier. Furthermore, there is nothing here specifically on Politics and international relations, or Politics and third-world studies, or Politics and feminism, for instance. Nor will readers find anything much about *methods* of political analysis, such as systemic or quantitative approaches, although some chapters do raise important methodological issues. Nonetheless, it is probably true to say – and some authors do say it – that these more or less specialized areas or methodologies might be taught or examined in the light of some or all of the general conceptions of politics they advance. They would, in short, represent particular case studies and illustrations of these general conceptions and approaches, and would be treated (or not treated as the case may be) in the light of them.

For example, because women have in general remained outside, or been excluded from, the *public* arena, their role and treatment in society has not been conceived of or studied as a *political* question. There are, for instance, very few undergraduate courses in Politics in which the issues that have been raised by feminist writers over the last twenty years are explored. These issues include both 'public' and 'private' ones, such as: the assumptions and policies of governments, managements and unions about women and work; the role and pay of women in the labour force; the framing of official governmental and private institutional policies as they affect women; debates about changes in the development of the welfare state in Britain (for instance, what sorts of benefits are needed, how much they should be and to whom they should be paid); socialization and opportunity patterns which affect the life-chances of women; violence against women in and outside the home – and so on.

The general absence of these issues from Politics courses may be explained in terms of a number of possibly interlinked factors: that the discipline of Politics has mainly been taught by men; that men have dominated formal public political life; that the dominant conceptions of politics have focused on this official or public realm of government and associated activities; that few of the great theorists have devoted major parts of their writing to issues which have been raised by feminists, although partial exceptions may be found in the work of, for example, Plato, Aristotle, J. S. Mill, Marx and Engels; and that the fragmentation of social science has meant that Sociology has in general been primarily concerned with the analysis of reproduction, family structure, socialization and related matters, and has hence appeared to be the natural home for gender studies. All this has acted to define such questions *out* of politics and Politics. And because the emphasis in Politics has been mainly on the government sector, so to speak, women have only really been 'noticed' politically when obtruding into the public arena (e.g. the suffragette movement, equal opportunity legislation and abortion pressure groups of one kind or another).[13]

---

[13] My thanks to Jane Morgan and Marian Sawer for helping to develop this point.

Now it will be clear from the following chapters that some of the conceptions of politics outlined there would tend to continue the exclusion of at least some of these issues from the discipline of Politics and others would not. The same would be true for the study of, for instance, 'race' relations – conventionally thought of as a 'sociological' question. And the study of international relations would be undertaken in the light of either the more institutionally tight focus of some conceptions of politics on the one hand, or the wider and more interdisciplinary conception of it in terms of the competitive struggle for control of or access to resources on the other hand. These differences represent not only distinctive theoretical approaches, but also distinctive conceptions of the stuff of politics itself.

8

Those coming to the discipline of Politics for the first time might be led to believe that the interesting diversity of views about politics in the following chapters is representative of the state of the discipline, and that they will encounter them in equal weight in their studies. This is not likely to be the case. For, as a number of the contributors point out in different ways, the fact of the matter is that *some* conceptions and approaches predominate in the discipline of Politics in Britain – and more widely as well. The conception of politics which predominates is that which regards it as largely confined to the official or public realm (that is an 'arena' or 'forum' approach). And the discipline of Politics has thus been organized around two broad focal areas. These are the study of the institutions of government and the state (including constitutional and political history, electoral studies, comparative government and administrative processes) on the one hand; and the study of political philosophy and theory (including the history of political thought, modern social and political theory plus the philosophy and some aspects of the methodology of social science) on the other hand. These focal concerns are still reflected in the names of certain departments or chairs at some of the older universities. For example, there are chairs of Social and Political Theory and of Government and Public Administration at Oxford; there are departments of Political Theory and Institutions (at Liverpool and Sheffield), of Political Theory and Government (at

Swansea), and of Government at Manchester and (alone amongst the 'new' universities) at Essex.

Now it is of course true that one may find many competing ways of studying these dominant concerns, and that a wide range of theories about these matters may be encountered by students in the liberal and social democracies. But this is not something which is found in many authoritarian societies in other parts of the world, past and present, where the banning (and burning) of books or the overtly political appointment and dismissal of lecturers is common.

So it is important for new students of Politics to recognize that there *is* a tradition within the discipline: some conceptions and approaches predominate, others are more marginal or are ignored. That is the nature of 'traditions' in this sense; that is the nature of disciplines and their conventions, as argued earlier. But there are times, as has been suggestively argued, when the dominating concerns, frameworks and theories of disciplines can no longer be sustained because they no longer engage with or satisfactorily explain the problems they are confronted with. When this happens – more or less quickly or cumulatively – there may commence a process which has been called a 'scientific revolution', when new conceptions, frameworks and theories emerge; when a new tradition or convention replaces the old.[14]

The development of the current tradition in the discipline of Politics, with its roots in Law, History (especially constitutional history) and Philosophy, has occurred mainly in the course of this century and in the years since the second world war especially.[15] The range of societies studied has clearly increased greatly over the period. And a variety of interesting innovations in ways of studying their government and politics has occurred. But the central concerns of the tradition within the discipline have not changed much, although a scatter of important subsidiary approaches and 'schools' have grown up around these.

Whether the discipline of Politics is approaching, or needs, a 'scientific revolution' are distinct questions. But they are ones which readers

[14] The notion of the 'scientific revolution' and its character has been most provocatively developed in Thomas Kuhn, *The Structure of Scientific Revolutions* (Chicago and London, 1970). It is not an uncontroversial thesis and has many critics. But it remains, for my money, a very suggestive approach for understanding many aspects of disciplines.

[15] A useful account of these developments in the discipline of Politics may be found in W. J. M. Mackenzie, *Politics and Social Science* (Harmondsworth, 1967), Parts 1 and 2. For some interesting personal – and sometimes rather bleak – reminiscences of major figures in Politics over the last twenty-five years, see the special issue of *Government and Opposition* 15(3/4) (1982), entitled *A Generation of Political Thought*.

of this book might find it useful to think about in the light of the contributions which follow. For the debate at York which gave rise to this book might be interpreted as uneasiness, at least amongst some local practitioners within the discipline of Politics, that its dominant conceptions and approaches no longer represent an adequate analytical and pedagogic response to the problems and politics of the world. The reorganization of the SSRC and its recent identification of research priorities may – to hang on to the metaphor – represent something of a 'counter-revolution', higher up.

Students and teachers who are concerned to promote a 'scientific revolution' in Politics will, as argued earlier, find it a very political affair. It is important to bear in mind that, as with all such pre-revolutionary or revolutionary situations, by no means everyone shares the same sense of unease about the discipline, and this is true for at least some of the contributors to this volume. Moreover, the continuation of the dominant tradition in teaching and research is anchored in a complex of broader academic, political and organizational relations within the universities and beyond them, linking up with a lattice of institutions and outlooks more widely in the state and society – and the point about the SSRC illustrates this clearly. All these, then, constitute the context, the web of circumstances, within which we all operate and in terms of which – and against which – change, if desired or necessary, will have to take place.

Perhaps it is worth concluding this Introduction by asking whether the current co-ordinates of the disciplinary map of Politics are adequate and appropriate, or whether they need to be substantially adjusted? The contributors to this volume would answer that question in very different ways. But, if the intellectual and pedagogic map of Politics *does* enable us to get somewhere in understanding and resolving political problems in human societies then perhaps we ought to praise current traditions and the SSRC – and pass out the old text-books. If not, a lot of redrawing of lines will be required. In answering this question much will depend on how we answer the other question: what is politics? The essays in this book may help readers to come to their own conclusions about both these questions in the light of their own work, thinking and experience.

1

Politics is about government

GRAEME C. MOODIE

1

When I began to study Politics, in the 1940s, at one of the relatively few British universities then to recognize it as a subject, it was divided into two broad sections: political theory and political institutions. Under the first head I was introduced to a handful of books in which major past thinkers (Plato, Hobbes, Locke and Rousseau) had reflected upon the nature of political society and the proper relations between rulers and ruled. The political institutions under that label were the most important visible organs of central (and to a lesser extent, local) government in Britain, the USA and the already defunct French Third Republic (representing, between them, advanced western democracy). Neither study was exclusively concerned with ideals and values or with facts: but political theory could be termed 'normative', in that it was largely about standards of judgement, and political institutions as 'empirical' in that it set out to describe actual institutions (like parliaments, cabinets and presidents) and their workings, albeit on the assumption that representative democracy was the most interesting, because most desirable, system of government.

This kind of Politics was particularly associated with the University of Oxford where it drew nourishment from the traditional and immensely powerful disciplines of History, Law and Philosophy. Elsewhere, and especially in the London School of Economics, attempts had been made to link Politics more closely with Psychology, Economics and Sociology, and to shift the empirical focus more to human behaviour and the solution of wide social problems – perhaps the most famous of the earlier arguments being those put forward by

Graham Wallas in his *Human Nature in Politics.*[1]

As a subject, at least as seen through the eyes of an undergraduate, Politics was remarkably unselfconscious. It seemed simply to take for granted that it required no distinctive method of enquiry, but could borrow, as appropriate or necessary, from the disciplines we have already mentioned, for all that Wallas (and later George Catlin[2]) tried to inculcate greater rigour on the empirical side. Nor was much attention given to the question on the title-page of this book – political activity, it seemed, like Politics, was centred upon the state and no further argument was required.[3]

In the years since the second world war it has become ever more widely accepted that the older preoccupation with political institutions (and I will now concern myself primarily with the more empirical aspects of Politics) could at best form only part of the search for political understanding. Wider definitions of the subject have been put forward, in particular, by two major if antagonistic schools of thought. The older school defines politics within the whole context of Marxist theory, a context of class conflict and the primacy of economic forces in which the state is allocated a secondary and derivative role (about the precise nature of which debate among Marxist thinkers is fierce and continuous).[4] The more recent approach, associated with American Political Science, focuses attention on the political *behaviour* of leaders and led, elites and masses, analysed within a wide variety of contexts inspired by other social sciences (including Economics and Cybernetics, for example). The type of behaviour regarded as political is defined by reference not so much to the state or government, as to certain functions or activities leading to 'the authoritative allocation of values' within and for a society,[5] or significantly concerned with 'power, rule or authority'.[6]

I do not find either view of politics entirely satisfactory. The Marxist one seems to imply either that Politics is merged into the one Marxist social science, or that its subject matter is of relatively little importance – but in any case cannot fully commend itself to a non-

---

[1] Published in London, 1908, and since reissued on several occasions with only minor changes.

[2] See, for example, his *The Science and Method of Politics* (London and New York, 1927); and *A Study of the Principles of Politics* (London and New York, 1930).

[3] For a modern restatement of this view see D. D. Raphael, *Problems of Political Philosophy* (London, 1970), ch. 1.

[4] See chapter 7 by Alex Callinicos in the present volume.

[5] See David Easton, *A Systems Analysis of Political Life* (New York, 1965).

[6] See Robert A. Dahl, *Modern Political Analysis* (Englewood Cliffs, New Jersey, 1963).

Marxist. The American behavioural emphasis is, to my mind, more attractive in principle, but it is not a single approach; and while in some forms it too can leave Politics as a mere subdivision of some over-arching social theory, in other forms it suffers rather from the lack of any clear boundaries or focus. Attempts to define politics in terms of the allocation of values or resources, for example, seem to me to be particularly vulnerable to this last objection, since that allocation is the outcome of the entire material and human aspects of society. It may well be true that the fullest understanding of the political (however defined), as of anything else in human life, would involve total knowledge of every aspect of that life – but the subject has to be manageable, as well as broader than merely the study of political institutions.

In everyday conversation the word 'politics' carries many associations. Political parties and leaders, elections and some aspects of government obviously enter the picture. But it also involves notions of persuasion, office-seeking, soliciting favour or support, compromise and (more disapprovingly) manipulation, duplicity, unprincipled bargaining and unscrupulous personal or sectional ambition. Ordinary usage is thus somewhat diverse in its connotations, but in common with other usages it at least provides room for two elements that I believe to be essential to the existence and nature of politics – government and conflict. It is these ideas, inseparably involved in the concept of governing, that also form the central subject-matter of the discipline of Politics.

This interpretation of both Politics and politics is open to dispute, but that is not the same thing as being vulnerable to criticism. I hope, in any case, that the attractions of the interpretation will manifest themselves as I offer an account of government and of the special kinds of conflict that lie at the heart of political activity.

2

When people in Britain talk about government they are usually referring either to *the* government, i.e. the people and organs of central government (the Cabinet, sometimes along with Parliament, the civil service, and so on), or to the way in which these people and organs are organized to form a system of, for example, democratic or elite government. The distinction between a particular government and the form or method of government is both clear and useful. Less commonly, people go on to distinguish both of them from government in the sense of the activity, that is, of governing. This distinction is nevertheless also of value, because not every activity of government can usefully be thought of as governing (selling an admission ticket to an ancient building, for example), nor is every instance of governing carried out by bodies normally considered to form part of the government.[7] More than that, in many societies that are undoubtedly governed there are no immediately identifiable governmental arrangements.[8]

To govern, broadly speaking, is to regulate or to control behaviour. In this broad sense governing is an inescapable feature of any enduring social grouping. Whether it is a family, a tribe, a nation-state, or a supranational entity like the European Economic Community (EEC), it can neither hang together nor cope with its environment unless its members' behaviour is sufficiently regular to permit communication, mutual adjustment and at least a minimum amount of co-operation. Many of the relevant patterns of behaviour must be learned, either in the normal course of growing up or, as with adult immigrants, through special induction procedures. Such induction processes are provided also for entrants into many private associations ranging from the Freemasons and churches to skilled trades and professions. Often, these patterns of behaviour are expressed as rules (of good manners, of morality, or about how to succeed, for example); even of those that are not, most can be put in the form of rules and will be for purposes of instruction. Thus Simon Roberts has pointed out that, among other things, 'in any society there must necessarily be some patterns of habitual conduct followed by the members,' even if in some small-scale ones people 'do not always think in terms of rules and obligations'.[9] Nevertheless, he adds, 'it does not follow that because people do not talk about rules they are unimportant.' (Throughout, he and we are discussing normative, prescriptive rules, and not the so-called scientific 'laws of nature' that are merely descriptive.)

Many of those rules originate in customs, which is to say that their

[7] For a brief discussion of these and another general sense of 'government', see S. E. Finer, *Comparative Government* (Harmondsworth, 1974), pp. 4-6.
[8] See Simon Roberts, *Order and Dispute: An Introduction to Legal Anthropology* (Harmondsworth, 1979); or, for example, M. Fortes and E. E. Evans-Pritchard (eds), *African Political Systems* (Oxford, 1940).
[9] See Robers, *Order and Dispute*, pp. 25-34.

precise origin is unknown, whereas others have been explicitly formulated by identifiable people or institutions (judges, committees, kings or parliaments, for example). In large modern complex societies this last category of rule plays a major and apparently increasing role, and we take it for granted that the elaborate division of labour and specialization of function on which such societies are based extends even to the business of making and applying rules. Clubs, trade unions, business companies, churches, schools, and all manner of other associations also have their governing bodies, committees, councils and conferences that make and remake the rules and supervise their application. Without such bodies these groupings would find it difficult or impossible to respond to changes in their condition or circumstances. This is true, above all, of those governing institutions that make and apply the most explicit, solemnly enforced and wide-ranging rules, the *legal* rules and regulations of a society.

Here we have the first major characteristic of governing: rule-making and applying. It follows that one defining feature of *the* government is that it is the body or set of bodies charged with the task of making certain rules, the laws, that claim and are normally accorded precedence over rules from other sources within that society. Conversely, where there is no such distinctive body we can say that there is no government (in that sense), as anthropologists say of some societies, even though the society is governed and its rules may change (however slowly). It is arguable even that rule-making is *the* defining element in government, but it is more useful to make separate mention of policy-making and implementation as additional distinctive aspects of government.

A policy may be defined as a programme of action (or inaction) adopted to further some purpose or to deal with some particular problem(s). (In some contexts it is very important to distinguish the formal adoption of a policy, that is, the declared intention to carry through a particular programme, from the course of action actually followed. The latter may well differ from the former through error, failures, inadvertence and so on, as successive governments demonstrated in the economic sphere during the 1970s. In some cases, too, governments may have no clear or coherent intentions, but actions will still be taken that, at least to the observer, may constitute the government's policy. But our present discussion is unaffected by the distinction.)

To plan and carry through such a programme for or on behalf of any

ALBRIGHT COLLEGE LIBRARY 194160

group is clearly an aspect of governing, and one that can usefully be distinguished from rule-making. The two activities may, of course, overlap to the extent that a particular policy may require new rules, or changes in old rules, if it is properly to be implemented. But the activities are nevertheless distinct, for governments also implement policies by other means (they give orders or try to persuade, for example), and policy-making is not the exclusive preserve of the official governing bodies. Admittedly, the latter may have formally to adopt and implement certain policies for them to be effective, but even in dictatorships policies do not always (if ever) spring fully fledged from the heads only of those in government office. Policies, like laws, draw their inspiration from many quarters, and the more democratic and liberal a society the greater the number of people and organizations likely to play some part in their formulation. Policy-making and implementing thus form other key components of the activity of governing.

A rule is in some sense binding or obligatory. Often, but not invariably, a rule is simply accepted as such and, therefore, complied with by those who come within its scope. But 'there is no society where rules are automatically obeyed,' [10] or not all the rules all the time; and, in consequence, sanctions are attached to most rules and non-observance brings a cost or penalty (though not necessarily a punishment). Even were compliance entirely voluntary, as in an ideal anarchist society, or in many games, rules would nevertheless not be self-applying. Even in a game, for example, the major task of an umpire or referee is to decide what rules mean and whether in fact they are infringed, rather than enforce them by the threat or application of sanctions.

Policies may also be said to bind the members of a group, quite apart from the obligations carried by any rules associated with them. Policies bind in the peculiar sense that for a group to carry out one policy or set of policies in any one area is to exclude every other policy or set of policies. No member or section of the group can simultaneously follow a different line and remain in the group: the parents send their children to a private school or a state one, not both; a nomadic tribe moves to a new hunting ground or it stays put a while longer, not both; the state puts the oil industry into public ownership or leaves it in other hands, not both; and the EEC either has a common agricultural policy or not, not both. Of course, a group may decide upon a policy of diversity in spheres of action where this is possible, and policy commitments can be

[10]   Lucy Mair, *Primitive Government* (Harmondsworth, 1962).

resisted or defied, perhaps successfully. If so, the policy will effectually have been changed and the new, changed policy becomes 'binding'.

It is beyond belief that a group could survive without rules or common policies (however made), but it is at least conceivable (however unlikely) that the members of a group might be so understanding, self-controlled and committed that loyalty and conscience sufficed to ensure the regularities and co-operation necessary for survival as a cohesive unit. Many have tried, ranging from the early Christian communities of the first few centuries AD to the rationalist 'utopias' of the nineteenth century or the 'hippy' communes of the 1960s in New Mexico. Very few survived for long. Normally, therefore, governing bodies attach explicit sanctions to their rules and policies. Threats and penalties may not be intrinsic to governing, but in practice they seem invariably to accompany it, and the right of exclusion from the group exists even in the host of angels in Heaven (according to some authorities).[11]

For this reason, among others, many have identified power as the hallmark of government. Maurice Duverger, for example, says that government means 'organized power, the institutions of command and control'.[12] A similar view constitutes at least one strand in Marxist and, especially, Leninist verdicts on the modern state: the state is seen as 'public power', a standing army and the police being the chief manifestations of its essential role as a 'special repressive force'.[13]

Resort to coercion, which is what power is often taken to mean, is not inherent in the very idea of governing (or there would be less dispute about its role); but if one defines power more generally to mean 'the ability to produce intended effects',[14] then it is an inescapable attribute of any effective government. If governments are to make rules and policies for a group or society, if they are to organize common services as they do now to an ever increasing extent (services ranging from defence to communications and the supply of energy, education, welfare and sports), they must be able to secure the co-operation and acquiescence of even the unwilling members of the society in question.

The exercise of power is thus an empirically, if not logically,

[11] See, among other sources, John Milton, *Paradise Lost*.
[12] Maurice Duverger, *The Idea of Politics: The Uses of Power in Society* (London, 1966), p. ix.
[13] See, in particular, V. I. Lenin, *State and Revolution*, first published in 1917. Modern commentators call attention to other characteristics as well as that of repressive class rule; see, for example, Michael Evans, *Karl Marx* (London, 1975), pp. 110-22; or George Lichtheim, *Marxism* (London, 1961), especially pp. 373-9.
[14] See Bertrand Russell, *Power* (London, 1960).

necessary aspect of governing, but its possession is not in itself a quality that distinguishes governments from the multitude of other organizations, groups and even individuals who also exercise power in some areas and to some degree, often in resistance to government. Nevertheless, the kind and extent of power wielded by the nation-state is one of the reasons for its importance and for the emphasis conventionally placed upon central governments in the study of politics.

3

Even in the most liberal of modern states central government is expected to have greater power than rival bodies within its territory, though not necessarily greater than the power available to all private organizations were they to work together. Moreover, it is seen to be the duty of the central government to direct and mobilize the resources of the community whenever they are needed to meet the threats or seize the opportunities presented by any important challenge; and if it fails, no other body in modern states is normally equipped to act in its place. The government, in other words, must represent and direct public power. (This is so important a feature of the modern state that Hannah Arendt even insists that the term 'power' should refer exclusively to it. 'Power', she writes, 'corresponds to the human ability not just to act but to act in concert. Power is never the property of an individual; it belongs to a group and remains in existence only so long as the group keeps together.' It should not be confused, she argues, with strength or violence.[15] In common with most political scientists, I have used 'power' as the generic term; but Arendt's sense, which I have referred to as public power, is a crucial species.)

Another important element in the power of central government is the general belief that it must 'uphold a claim to the exclusive regulation of the legitimate use of physical force' within its own territory, to quote Robert Dahl.[16] Private armies, private vengeance and other types of private force must at least be subject to public control if they cannot always be prevented. For all that it is misleading to say that government

[15] See her essay 'On Violence' in her *Crises of the Republic* (Harmondsworth, 1973), pp. 83-146. The quotation is from p. 113.
[16] See his *Modern Political Analysis*, p. 12. He was modifying a well-known definition of the state by Max Weber in his *The Theory of Social and Economic Organization* (Oxford, 1947), p. 154. And also see chapter 2 by Peter Nicholson in the present volume.

means 'organized power', it is thus undeniable that power is one crucial aspect of government – but only one; even Marx refers also to 'common activities (of the state) arising from the nature of all communities'.[17]

Among the other important features that explain (and justify) the attention given to central governments are: their scope, in terms both of the numbers of people affected by their decisions and of the areas of life coming under their jurisdiction; and, above all, the widespread belief that they have the authority or right, and not merely the power, to assert themselves in areas denied to others.

How governments are organized and go about their business, who serves in them and how and why, and what they do are clearly matters of importance. So too are questions about the kinds of problem they face, the major influences to which they are subject, and the criteria by which they should be judged. Nor must one omit from this catalogue the impact on behaviour and events of political institutions like the electoral system (which, in the British general election of 1983, for example, translated a minority of the popular vote into a large majority of Parliamentary seats). What may be less clear is what government (governments and governing) has to do with politics.

J. D. B. Miller provides part of the answer when he writes that 'government is the arena of *politics*, the prize of politics, and, historically speaking, the residue of past politics.'[18] He goes on to say that 'there are parts of it in which the political element is hardly noticeable,' a reference to the fact that much of the work of government, especially as spokesman or provider of services, is formal or routine and in any case quite uncontroversial. Politics, as we will now argue, is none of these things.

Governments, as we have seen, constitute the more deliberate and purposeful elements in the process of governing but, as we have also noted, they are by no means the only sources of the policies they adopt and seek to implement. Nor are they always of one mind. About the nature of these policies there is no necessary or automatic agreement within or outside governments any more than there usually is about who should compose (in Britain) the Cabinet, the House of Commons or other governing bodies responsible for them. On the contrary, for a number of reasons disagreement and conflict are to be expected in any

[17] See his *Capital*, III (Moscow, 1962), pp. 376-7, cited in Evans, *Karl Marx*, p. 114.

[18] J. D. B. Miller, *The Nature of Politics* (Harmondsworth, 1962), p. 19. Emphasis not in the original.

society. Fundamentally, disagreement about social and governmental matters is rooted in two ineradicable features of human life. The first is that we want the same things, but not all of us can have them. This is obviously true of scarce economic resources like oil-wells, food-stuffs, and accommodation in exclusive residential areas, which we are accustomed to have allocated through the economic market, or even of things like city-centre parking, unimpeded access to places of special beauty like England's Lake District or New England's Cape Cod without their being spoiled by crowds of other people, which *could* be allocated through the price mechanism (that is, rationed through the purse by charging a sufficiently high price for admission) but rarely are. It is also true of quite different things, like being top dog (whether as the fastest runner, prima ballerina or president), a setter of standards, a successful entertainer or a Nobel Peace Prize winner, none of which could ever be secured merely by tendering money.

The second root of conflict is that we also want different things, and not all our wants are fully compatible. Some such conflicts, as between a farmer and a house-builder for the same piece of land, are but further manifestations of the first problem; but in Britain and most other countries land-use has been subjected to government regulation and thus in part removed from the economic market. Other, more generalised conflicts also derive from material scarcity, but today tend to be even more matters for governmental decisions. They include the mutually incompatible aims of advocates of lower taxation and beneficiaries of public expenditure, property developers and conservationists, or 'organic' farmers and the sellers of artificial fertiliser.

In a different category lie such other familiar disputes as those over the 'rights' to privacy or silence as opposed, say, to the 'rights' to public knowledge or to play the trombone, over cigarette smoking in public places, or over the best *methods* of distributing or producing wealth, none of which derive directly from economic scarcity. Given that we are talking of physical goods, of services *and* of positions of pre-eminence, etc., it is worth stressing that the fact of scarcity is not dependent on particular social or economic systems but is an inherent element in human existence and derives at least in part from the fact that human life is itself limited in space and time. (It is for this reason that the Marxist vision of total abundance and harmony must be condemned as illusory).

In this last group of cases we re-encounter precisely the situation that, we suggested earlier, makes a policy 'binding': the fact that one policy or allocation necessarily excludes all others. And it is in this situation that one most clearly encounters what S. E. Finer has called 'the political predicament'.[19]

The political predicament may best be understood by reference to three elements. The first is that some decision on common action is required (e.g. a policy must be adopted or a leader chosen) if a social unit is to deal with some problem or adapt to a new or changed situation. The second is that there is disagreement as to what that policy or choice ought to be, a disagreement made all the sharper by the knowledge that it will bind those who are opposed as well as those who are in favour. The third is that both the policy or leader chosen and the processes of selection from a range of possibilities must be such as to permit the unit or grouping to survive as a unit. If, for example, disagreement could always be satisfactorily coped with by the group's splitting into two or more separate units, each with its own policies and leaders, there would be no real predicament. But in fact a combination of calculation (that 'unity is strength,' for example), sentiment (nationalist feeling, for example), the need for defensible frontiers, and, often, the inextricable social intertwining of the various groups, means that a high value is placed upon continuing cohesion and to split up is, therefore, usually regarded as a sign of failure, or even as an act of collective treachery that must be resisted, if necessary by force, as it was in the American civil war.

The activities required to cope with the predicament, the mixture of pressures and other kinds of persuasion needed to secure sufficient agreement for a leader to emerge or a policy to be adopted and implemented, these are what I call politics. (A politician, it may be added to round off this account, is one who is regularly and actively involved in this process and, more popularly, one who seeks governmental office through the support of others and thereby seeks to shape policy; and to the extent that his success depends on the bringing together of antagonistic people and interests, the reputation for (even the fact of) slipperiness may be as understandable as the inevitability of compromise.)

To avoid misunderstanding, it should be stressed that not all disputes in society give rise to politics or constitute political problems. Many disputes are too trivial, even though they may relate to a governmental

[19] In the first chapter of his *Comparative Government*, to mention only the most accessible source. Compare J. D. B. Miller's use of the phrase 'political situation' in *The Nature of Politics*, p. 14.

decision – the typeface used on government writing-paper, for example. Others are purely private; whether you prefer butter or margarine, or rock to jazz, for example, since no issue of common action is raised unless one of them is to be banned, subsidised or made compulsory. Yet other disputes may not present a political problem because they are soluble by reference to already agreed means, whether by reference to a final arbitrator or by using scientific procedures or some other mechanism accepted in a particular society.

None of these categories, of course, is permanently non-political: exactly what is trivial, private or soluble by agreed and non-contentious procedures is itself open to dispute in principle and may at any time become an issue; though no society can expect easily to survive in which these are constant matters of intense and widespread disagreement.

It is often asked why all problems are not dealt with by agreed procedures and thus, as it is sometimes said, 'taken out of politics'. To that question there are two principal answers. The first and rather 'Pickwickian' one is that in some degree they already are in any stable society. Any enduring set of basic rules about how governments shall be organized and operate, any working constitutions that is to say, and all political institutions (not only parliaments, but also parties and some pressure groups) together and separately are just that: agreed procedures for dealing with political problems. And, in Britain, for example, they in fact deal with them in the sense of helping to define, channelize and contain conflict sufficiently, most of the time, for most people to accept most of the policies and choices that emerge.

That Britain's political institutions have been even relatively successful may partly be a matter of good fortune, but it is also a result of deliberate and perceptive effort by generations of political actors and observers. To know the procedures that help to define the game of politics and thus to participate effectively is in itself a sufficient justification for the study of institutions; but we also need to understand why those institutions operate as they do and how they relate to the structures and forces of the wider social environment (which is what contemporary students of politics attempt to do).

Political procedures and institutions are thus important aspects of government, but of themselves they cannot resolve every problem nor provide a certain road to social harmony. This is so because of their own inadequacies – some of which may be remediable, sometimes in ways advocated by scholars. But harmony is elusive also and mainly because of the very nature of the most distinctive and persistent issues to appear on the agenda of government – issues about which disagreement is legitimate and which are both too serious to leave to chance or individual preference and too complex and difficult to resolve by reference to any principle of certainty. They cannot, therefore, properly and appropriately be dealt with either by science or, for example, by the mere counting of votes: instead they can and must be matters of judgement. There are, for example, no indisputable and unambiguous tests for deciding on the 'correct' penalties for murder, the best pattern of organization of an industry, or the one fair system of rewards for labour, but all of these are too important to be settled arbitrarily with no reference at all to the relevant evidence or arguments. Hence the need for judgement.

Human judgement is clearly fallible, and thus its use is rarely undisputed, but it is nevertheless capable of improvement through training and experience, and it may be recognizably well or ill founded. Its exercise is in any case unavoidable when full knowledge of important matters is unavailable, because whim or personal taste would be an inadequate and irresponsible ground for decision, and because important values or ends, themselves derived neither from full knowledge nor from individual preference alone, are inescapably involved. This is both the second major reason why agreed procedures cannot settle every dispute and the final defining characteristic of politics. It has been aptly and authoritatively expressed by Hanna Pitkin:

> Political questions . . . are questions about action, about what should be done; consequently they involve both facts and value commitments, both ends and means. And, characteristically, the factual judgements, the value commitments, the ends and the means, are inextricably intertwined in political life . . . . Politics abounds with issues on which men are committed in a way that is not easily accessible to rational argument. Yet, at the same time, rational arguments are sometimes relevant, and agreement can sometimes be reached. Political life . . . is always a combination of bargaining and compromise where there are irresolute and conflicting commitments, and common deliberation about public policy, to which facts and rational arguments are relevant. [20]

[20] H. F. Pitkin, *The Concept of Represenation* (Berkeley, California, 1967 and 1972, p. 212. Compare also Eric (Lord) Ashby, 'The Scientist as University President' in his *Adapting Universities to a Technological Society* (San Francisco and London, 1974), pp. 88-102.

4

There can, I think, be no dispute about the reality or importance of this kind of predicament and of the conflicts to which it gives rise. Nor, I suggest, can it be denied that such predicaments are inseparable from the work of government. In addition, I have been arguing, they also serve to define the essential nature and purpose of political activity in every enduring human group or association, and most conspicuously the state. If this be granted, then we can summarize the consequent view of Politics by saying that it is the study of how men handle controversial issues which cannot be settled simply by resort to rational argument and indisputable evidence. It involves analysing those unavoidable predicaments, faced everywhere, which stem from man's dependence upon other men who have different interests and wishes as well as much in common. The focal point of both the study and the activities studied is government, which is to say, the unending task of making the changing rules and policies for any human society so that it may survive.

2

Politics and force

PETER P. NICHOLSON

THE QUESTION AT ISSUE

There are several basic questions about the study of politics, and I am concerned with only one of them. Which human actions constitute 'politics' – what is the subject-matter which the academic discipline of Politics studies? This is a question about the province of Politics, and it asks what is to count as 'political' and what is not. It seems a simple question, until one tries to answer it. We normally think, for instance, that art or literature is different from politics: but how does one explain what the difference is? Besides, there are occasions when art or literature *is* political, and falls within the province of Politics – which is why paintings or books are sometimes banned by governments, as in Nazi Germany, Soviet Russia, and even Britain. In what respect, exactly, might works of art and literature be political? In other cases, moreover, there is on all occasions controversy about whether something is politics or not. Is economic activity, for example, political? That there are usually separate university departments of Economics and Politics is, of course, inconclusive; as is the fact that Politics used often to be taught as part of Economics.

The question about the boundary of Politics can be distinguished from another question, which asks 'what is politics?' – what is the nature or the characteristic feature of politics? If certain activities are to be grouped together as 'political', how then are they to be described? Is politics the art of the possible, a dirty business, 'who gets what, when and how?', the resolution of conflict, or what? This question and my question are closely related. In order to answer my question, one needs to have at least some idea of what kind of activity politics is, or one does not know where to start. It is not necessary, however, to have a comprehensive or fully developed theory. The first step is simply to identify what is political and should be the material for the student of Politics: better understanding of its nature and characteristics comes later. In the same way, it is legitimate to say that the subject-matter of biology is life before one knows all the life-forms there are or have been, and before one knows about their structure and behaviour. At this level, the aim is to set the boundaries to an area for study, not to state the conclusions that emerge from its study.

I ignore totally another related question, concerning the proper method for studying politics. This is often raised in the form 'Can there be a science of Politics?' It involves matters I do not need to cover, and I shall not discuss it at all. The other question, about the nature of politics, I shall discuss as little as possible. Nonetheless, both questions are worth mentioning because they show the great importance of my main question about determining the province of Politics. Where we fix the boundaries will be a major factor in how we deal with the other two questions. Both what we construct as the best method for the study of politics and what we conclude about its nature depend upon which activities we decide are political. Obviously, we must know what is to be studied before we can sensibly decide which is the best way to study it, or reach any well-grounded conclusions about its characteristics. Therefore I concentrate on the question about boundaries because it is logically prior, that is, must be answered first.

As political philosophy is the branch of Politics with which I am most familiar, I approach the question from its perspective. This does not mean I feel free to indulge in armchair theorizing and to do without facts. The facts of politics are the raw data of political philosophers as of any student of politics, and much of my argument is illustrated by specific examples. Political philosophy can also, however, be very abstract, because it reflects upon politics, and Politics, at the most general level. In particular, it investigates the most basic assumptions being made by students of politics. Accordingly, I examine some abstract theoretical matters about what is involved in answering this kind of question about 'the political'; but I shall leave that until last, when it should have become clearer anyway. First I state my dissatisfaction with some of the ways in which it has been suggested that the boundary of politics can be fixed, and offer an alternative, explaining why I think it is better. I aim to present a stark outline of my position, and to assert it polemically against other views. Qualifications are kept to a minimum, so that the crucial differences of opinion are sketched as sharply as possible, and the reader is offered a clear alternative to set alongside other views. At the end of the paper, when I consider what special contribution political philosophy can make, I give my own reflections on how to react to being faced with different answers to the question.

SOME UNSATISFACTORY ANSWERS

Human activity does not come labelled 'political' or 'non-political'. Students of politics must themselves choose what is to count as political, thereby setting the limits to Politics. The subject is not unique: every discipline has to determine its own boundaries, for example, History, Chemistry or English. Some disciplines, notably in the natural sciences, have sharp and distinct edges, with all or most of their practioners agreeing upon them. Politics, however, like many of the humanities and social studies, does not. Many different and even divergent ways of delimiting the discipline have been suggested, and there is no consensus upon where its boundary runs. Consider these instances: the House of Commons debating a Bill, an American ambassador mediating between warring states in the Middle East, elders fixing the day a nomadic tribe should move on to the next pasture, salesmen wondering how to counter a rival's advertising campaign, members of a trade union voting for a new secretary, Britain's National Trust leasing land to the Ministry of Defence, a man beating his slave, a priest giving a sermon, a family deciding whether to have a holiday abroad this year, and a small boy pleading with his sister to buy him an ice-cream. Which of these are, or in certain circumstances might be, instances of politics? It would be an exaggeration to say that no two professional students of politics would agree on the answer, but one could easily find two who did not. Some would accept everything on this list as being political, others would exclude some; and which were excluded would vary considerably from one person to another.

No student of Politics, therefore, can avoid making his or her own choice of a definition of politics – and it is better that it is done consciously and explicitly. Some of the answers which have been offered are clearly unsatisfactory. We want a criterion of the political which is comprehensive, distinctive and fruitful. It must include all politics, exclude everything else, and suggest areas for research. Some definitions fail because they include too little and exclude too much, while others fail because they include too much and exclude too little; in either case, they conceal, block or render unmanageable lines of enquiry which Politics students ought to pursue. It is helpful to examine some inadequate definitions because it illustrates the difficulties and pitfalls and teaches the requirements which a more satisfactory definition must meet.

It is, for example, too narrow to define politics in terms of conflict between social classes. If the student of politics takes class struggle as the criterion of the subject, then no society which does not contain classes will be looked at, thus cutting out material from so-called 'primitive' societies which might be very informative. Again, it will be assumed that if there are classes then there must be conflict between them, and that a society which abolishes classes will be free of conflict. These assumptions are contestable and, more important, they rule out certain lines of investigation. For instance, anyone who takes for granted that a classless society cannot have politics may miss signs indicating that, nonetheless, it persists. To put it another way, our assumption should be that politics is universal and occurs in all societies. This can be abandoned if we find a society without politics. But a definition which confines politics to a limited range of societies is suspect because it excludes from consideration the very cases which might overthrow it.

Sometimes politics is described as a particular way of settling issues. It is reaching decisions through rational discussion and argument leading to persuasion and assent, rather than through violence and compulsion. Some think that people can be free only where there is politics of that kind, and that it occurs only in truly representative democracy. This view of politics, whatever its merit as a political ideal, could never serve to set the limits to the study of Politics, because once again too much is excluded. We must take account of the workings of all cases of politics, not simply of those which we approve as morally good. Tyranny and dictatorship, imperialism and repression, all fall within the province of Politics, as well as democracy and free government. One will never understand a subject properly by looking at a biased sample of its material, whatever the source of the bias.

Some other approaches are inadequate because they are too wide. Suppose that we say politics is about disagreement, conflict and their resolution (by whatever means, peaceable or violent, autocratic or democratic). This might be challenged on a number of grounds; for example, it might be argued that politics is indeed about resolving conflict, but that it is also about much else besides, since there can be politics even when there is no conflict (surely an act of the legislature is political even if it settles no dispute but is passed unanimously and is desired by the whole population?). It can also be challenged, more fundamentally, for including too much. There are many cases of conflict which are nothing to do with politics: for instance, if two mathematicians contest a proof for squaring the circle, or if lovers quarrel. Students of politics are interested in that subclass of conflict and conflict-resolution which occurs within a political context. To define politics in terms of conflict is not enough, because we need a further criterion to tell us *which* conflicts. Several other definitions are vulnerable to the same charge of being too wide. Thus it is insufficient to say that politics is government – schools and banks have government too; or that it is the making of decisions – there are non-political decisions by groups and individuals; or that it is the allocation of resources – resources are allocated outside politics too, in businesses and in families, for instance. All these definitions fail to mark the distinction between what is politics and what is not, and hence present the student with such a vast field that it is hard to know where to begin.

A BETTER ANSWER: POLITICS AND FORCE

What we need, then, is a criterion for picking out what is distinctive of politics and occurs in all cases of politics. I believe that 'force' is the answer. To explain what I mean, I begin with modern states, which are of course only one type of political organisation, and then extend my treatment to international politics and to societies which are not states.

In a modern state, a particular body of people, the government, makes decisions, puts them into practice, adjudicates disputes, and generally runs and organizes the society. What makes the government's actions political, however, is not that they are general and may or do affect everyone in the society; after all, a manufacturer's decision is just as general when he fixes the price of his product. The distinctive mark of a political action is that it can be enforced, because the government can coerce people into obedience by the threat of physical force, and ultimately by using it. There are some very obvious instances of this. Governments make laws which tell its citizens to act, or to abstain from acting, in particular ways. These laws incorporate orders to officials to apprehend and punish those who disobey. That is, laws are sanctioned by force. This is true not only of criminal law, which lays down rules everyone must follow (e.g. do not injure others), but also of civil law, which offers us facilities to use or not as we wish (e.g. if you want to marry, this is how to). In the latter case, we need not avail ourselves of the law's services: but as soon as we do, we subject ourselves and others to the law and take on legal obligations whose performance we can be forced to render. For example, the person who marries can later be divorced, even against his or her will, and become liable to maintenance payments which can be extracted by force. It is not only criminals but also those who flout the judgements of civil courts who may feel the force of the law, having their property confiscated, or being imprisoned. Furthermore, there is a key class of laws, which varies in extent and content from state to state, solely concerned with securing the position of the state and of the government: laws covering treason, subversion, opposition, criticism, loyalty, official secrets, and so on. Every kind of law, administrative, constitutional or whatever, can be seen in the end, directly or indirectly, to involve the potential exercise of force.

It is true that making those sorts of laws is only one of the functions which the government of a modern state performs. It also provides all kinds of services for the members of its society, to do with health, housing, employment, education, and so on, and undertakes to defend them from external aggression. But in many cases the citizens are compelled to use these services, for instance, to send their children to school, to live only in housing which satisfies a certain standard, to be vaccinated, or to be defended against another state, or an internal enemy, with whom they may in fact sympathize. Once again the government may end up forcing people to do what they do not want to do. Furthermore, the government and all its activities have to be paid for, and this has to be done by the government taking for its own use resources which individuals would otherwise have possessed, for example by taxation. Taxation, one of the most ancient and basic features of government, is the forcible appropriation of individuals' property: some regard as forced labour the effort spent in earning the money to pay taxes.

In the modern state, the hands of the government are everywhere, and even when helping are still ready to clench into iron fists and coerce people. This is why politics is so important. We cannot avoid it: and it involves our being forced to do things, or to pay for things, which we may not wish to. Politics is about going to war with another state, financing a particular kind of defence armament, building a certain type of power station, giving overseas aid, joining international organizations, allowing women to have abortions, censoring videos, controlling the use of drugs and alcohol, permitting the practice of religions: and in every case what the government decides is what we are forced to do or to have, like it or not.

Of course, governments do not always actually resort to force. Their laws and policies may meet widespread approval and support. Moreover, it is very expensive and sometimes risky to force people, and governments usually prefer as far as possible to get their way by other means, for instance by deceit or by persuasion, so that their orders are routinely accepted and soldiers are replaced by bureaucrats. Often governments can rely upon goodwill built up over a long period, or can take advantage of passive acquiescence or inertia on most people's part. Every government takes care to present itself as legitimate, and nurses the general habit of obedience to authority which is so significant in politics. At the same time, every state contains its criminals, tax evaders, dissidents and traitors, and perhaps active rebels, and every government is using force against some of its subjects – usually a minority but sometimes a majority. Even when force is not used, it could be: its possible exercise is always there, and that is what is distinctive about politics.

Someone might counter that, in fact, other groups and individuals use force, as well as governments and their officials. What about rebels, armed robbers, or even a parent chastising – or battering – a child? This is a very important objection, because if it can be shown that there is private force as well as public force then 'force' is no more useful to distinguish politics than I have argued 'conflict' is, since we should still need a criterion of public, i.e. political, force. Now it is undeniable that others exercise force besides the government. Some do so illegitimately, against the government's orders, others do it with the government's permission. The two possibilities are covered by the formula devised by Max Weber, one of the most famous exponents of the view that force is the specifically political means of action. The modern state, according to Weber, successfully claims the monopoly of the legitimate use of physical force within its territory.[1] A government can be said successfully to claim the monopoly of the use of force because it controls crime and represses rebellion; and it can be said to monopolize the legitimate use of physical force because private individuals may use force only with its permission and within specified limits – for instance, parents for discipline, and boxers for sport. Sometimes a government has to fight hard to make good its claim, and sometimes the monopoly is lost; people break the law with impunity, or take its enforcement into their own hands, or rebels hold large tracts of territory (in which they are the government). There is disorder or civil war, and no effective government. Sooner or later, however, the government re-establishes itself, or else it disappears and a new government will emerge, or perhaps the territory of the old state will be replaced by two states, each with its own government. The possibilities can be readily observed in the contemporary world. Consider the civil strife and turmoil in recent years in the Congo (Katanga), Nigeria (Biafra), Cyprus, Ethiopia, Vietnam, Cambodia, Pakistan (Bangladesh), South America, Iran or the Lebanon. The crucial point is that in any one political organization and its territory there can be only one body in control, that is, able to use force successfully and beat off any challenges to it. This is where 'force' differs from 'conflict' as a criterion of politics. Ultimately there is not room for two or more exercisers of force, nor for superior and inferior force. By the very nature of force, only one body is able successfully to back its decisions by force; otherwise there is not a viable society, nor a political organization. The use of force in a society must form a unitary system. Hence force is always distinctive of politics, and always identifies the political. There can, on the other hand, be more than one kind of decision-making co-existing in the same society: but only those decisions which are backed by force are political.

Let me continue to compare my criterion of the political with those which I have rejected as inadequate. I have deliberately said nothing about the purpose for which force is used. It may be the basis of a tyrant's power, or enable a majority to oppress or exterminate a minority; or it may be the means by which a democratic government

---

[1] H. H. Gerth and C. Wright Mills (eds), *From Max Weber: Essays in Sociology* (New York, 1946), pp. 77-8; and Talcott Parsons (ed.), *Max Weber: The Theory of Social and Economic Organization* (New York, 1947), pp. 154-6. Weber has been influential: see, for example, Gabriel Almond in G. A. Almond and James S. Coleman (eds), *The Politics of the Developing Areas* (Princeton, 1960), pp. 5-7; and Robert A. Dahl, *Modern Political Analysis* (Englewood Cliffs, New Jersey, 1976), ch. one.

secures and protects the human rights of its citizens. It may be used by capitalist states or by socialist states; by governments which minimize their role in society, or by governments which maximize it. But whether the ends for which force is used are evil or good, and what the ideology of the state may be, is irrelevant. The mere fact that force is exercised suffices to establish that there is politics. This satisfies the requirement, laid down earlier, than no cases of politics be excluded on moral grounds. At the same time, the other requirement, that some social activity be excluded as non-political, is met too. Using force as our criterion enables us to discriminate between some decisions and others, counting as political only those which are about the use of force, involve its use, or are backed by it ultimately. We can discriminate in the same way between political and non-political conflicts, between political and non-political resolutions of conflict and between economic activities which are political and those which are not. We thereby exclude from Politics the study of the running of such groups and institutions as businesses, trades unions, schools, universities, banks, churches and families, because in none of them may force play a role except with the permission of the state. If force is employed in such a group without the state's permission, that is illegitimate, the victim can appeal to the state, and the state can make its decision stick.

Thus the definition of politics in terms of force is neither too narrow nor too wide. In addition, it prompts plenty of significant questions for Politics' research agenda. It focuses attention on the central feature that politics is always, at some point, a matter of some persons compelling others. It raises interesting questions about the means by which this can be done. For instance, how is force actually exercised? How do people organize themselves for this purpose, and what else is involved? Do those who exert force have to receive some support which is not itself extorted by the threat of force? How do small groups manage to dominate much larger ones? If force is so central, why are not all governments run by the military – how do civil politicians retain control? Are there limits to what can be achieved by force, and in particular by that intensive use of it termed 'terror'? For those concerned to recommend ways of improving political activity, it indicates that the use of force is inevitable and that the main issues are first, how to keep it under control and ensure that it is employed only for necessary and socially beneficial tasks, and second, how to decide which ends can properly be assigned to governments and can justify the use of force as a means to their achievement.

Next, I turn to the political relations between states. I think that many people would accept that these provide strong confirmation of the view I have been putting forward. There are agreements made between states, there are international bodies, there is international law, and there are international courts. But in the end each state is its own judge, and its own executor of the law, and disputes are still regularly settled by force. The only check on one state's use of force is its use or threatened use by another state or states. Force, therefore, is the central feature of international as of domestic politics. Indeed, force is even more prominent internationally, since it is used not only to enforce laws and rules, but also turned to as an alternative in those frequent cases where there are no rules regulating the relations between states. It is possible that in the future force might be used less, if the present multiplicity of sovereign states were replaced by a unitary world political organization. But I do not see that force would ever be eliminated. The world government would still need to enforce its decisions, to maintain order and peace, and to deal with dissidents, for example with those who wished to secede and form an independent state (with the danger that the process of wars between states would resume).

The last point I have to consider is whether, on my definition of politics, there is politics in societies which are not states. The societies which pose the largest problem for my account are those popularly called 'primitive' societies. They are also known as 'peoples without government', 'stateless societies', 'tribes without rulers' or, more strictly, 'acephalous' (literally, 'headless') societies. As these terms suggest, these societies – now virtually extinct – lacked the formal political institutions found in modern and earlier forms of the state. There was no body of persons which was the government, there was no civil service, no police, no army, and there were no courts. In some of these societies, usually the smaller ones (and they could be as small as 100 persons), there were not even any individuals who could be identified as politicians, policemen or judges: those very social roles seem not to have existed. Nonetheless, even in these extreme cases, I think we can say that there was politics. There were rules which everyone had to observe, and the rules were enforced, with banishment or death as ultimate sanctions. The difference is that enforcement was diffused instead of concentrated; that is, it was left to everyone and anyone to enforce the rules instead of that task being assigned to one individual as his office. Force was not absent, it simply ran along different channels.

To sum up the position I have been constructing, in any society force is used to settle certain conflicts, to sanction certain rules, to back certain decisions and to guaranteee that certain policies are pursued. The use and control of force by some members of the society, and the moves by others to influence their use of it, or to gain control of it for themselves, are the distinctively political human activities. On this view, there is politics in a society, and between societies, but almost never anywhere else. The groups of people *within* a society do not in themselves have politics, although they can become involved in politics. For example, when the members of a trade union choose their officials, or when officials negotiate rates of pay and conditions of work with employers, that is not politics: when, on the other hand, the union subscribes to a political party, or lobbies the government on the law relating to picketing, that is politics.

POLITICAL PHILOSOPHY'S CONTRIBUTION

What contribution can political philosophy make to the discussion of this question about defining the political and determining the boundaries of politics? political philosophy has several subdivisions, two of which are immediately relevant.

First, we can gain considerable help from the history of political thought which, among other things, traces the development of ideas about politics. Earlier writers have adopted their own views of what politics is, and many of them have emphasized force, for example, Thucydides, Aristotle, Machiavelli, Hobbes and Marx. Many too have considered the people's control of their rulers to be a central problem because of the dangers involved in having to put force at the government's disposal; Locke and Rousseau, for instance, the Federalists, and the Utilitarians (Bentham, and James and John Stuart Mill). Rather than look for writers who agree with one's view, however, it is more important to note that political thinkers over the past two and a half millennia have dealt with an extensive range of political systems, including oriental despotisms, city-states, the Roman Empire, the feudal kingdoms and Papacy of the Middle Ages, the early modern nation-state, and the various stages of the growth of the states we know today. These political systems differ enormously in size, social complexity, technological and economic level, and nature and extent of government activity. The ideas of the political thinkers who lived in them, both their political analyses and their statements of political ideals, cannot be properly understood save with reference to the conditions peculiar to their own times. It would be absurd, for example, to read Plato's attacks on Athenian direct democracy as if they were applicable without modification to modern mass democracy. Yet political philosophers seek to reach conclusions which are true for all time. The student of the history of political philosophy faces the stimulating and educational challenge of having to distinguish between ideas about politics which are ephemeral because they are based on transient historical circumstances, and those which penetrate to the permanent and essential.

In the second place, political philosophy includes the critical examination of the assumptions which we make as students of Politics. It reflects upon such problems of method as the present question of the definition of politics. The reader of this volume cannot but be struck by the great differences of opinion which exist as to the correct answer to this question. My own view, though I do not think it is universally held, is that it is a mistake to treat the question as having a 'correct' answer. Students of Politics disagree over the boundaries of their subject, and there is no way in which we can decide conclusively between their competing definitions. There is no yardstick by which to adjudicate between the different positions which are adopted, so that we can point to one as the correct answer. 'Politics' is a special kind of technical term, the kind that is definitive of the whole technique, that is, of the study of Politics, and technical terms are created by the practitioners of the technique. (Compare the case of 'Medicine'.) It is possible, and it happens, that different practitioners of Politics work with different definitions of the subject. There is no evidence that this has hindered the discipline, or that it is anything but a healthy condition which keeps basic issues alive and the road to new developments open. Moreover, there seems no good reason for trying to avoid this plurality of definitions by replacing it by a single, commonly adopted definition (the selection of which must be arbitrary).

Finally, what are the implications of that last point for my own answer to the question, which human activities constitute politics? I have claimed that we should study any society, including 'primitive' societies, on the assumption that it includes arrangements, usually a special set of institutions and social roles, for the regulation and use of force, and that these are the heart of politics. The arrangements can vary considerably from one society to another, and therefore Politics ought to be a comparative study gathering its material not only from the contemporary world but also from other historical periods and other cultures. In this way we can begin to locate the unchanging features of politics. I do not suggest that the study of force should constitute the whole of Politics, though I think it has to be central. I proffer my own view of politics in the spirit that it is one suggestion among many, and that the reader will be wise to set it alongside others and test them all out. Each, no doubt, will have its strengths and weaknesses and some may turn out to complement one another. Consequently one may conclude that it is best to deploy a combination of criteria of the political, either simultaneously or separately to suit particular circumstances. If this is a fair assessment of the situation, then clearly it is sensible to spread oneself across as broad a range of material and method as possible, so that one can make an informed choice among the various definitions of politics. It must be recognized that to a large extent the choice of one's own definition (or definitions) of politics cannot be the starting point but must be the product of one's study of Politics. Any initial definition should be adopted tentatively, tested, and possibly revised. It is very salutary that such open-mindedness is required of us. The most important lesson for all of us to learn is that it is a strength of Politics as a discipline that it contains many differing conceptions of itself and many frameworks for study, for the very process of coming to terms with them is itself instructive.

3

Politics as collective choice

ALBERT WEALE

AN EXAMPLE OF COLLECTIVE CHOICE

Once upon a time, not very long ago, the following incident occurred. The council of a city in the north of England discovered that it had a surplus on its housing revenue account. In the normal course of events this would mean a saving on the rates for the next year. However, the council might instead use the surplus to cut council house rents for the next year and keep the rates at their planned level. The decision would depend on political forces on the council. These forces were divided along party political lines. The Conservatives were the largest single group, but they did not have an overall majority. By combining their forces, the Labour and the Liberal councillors could outvote the Conservatives. Indeed any two parties voting together would always form a majority against the third.

The Labour group proposed that weekly council house rents should be reduced, a move which the Conservatives opposed in favour of keeping the cut in the rates. The Liberals proposed an amendment to Labour's proposition, suggesting that instead of a cut in the weekly rents, the tenants should pay the same rent but should be allowed two rent-free weeks. In other words, a majority of the council were in favour of using the surplus to reduce the amount that council tenants paid, rather than use the money to cut rates. Yet, when it came to the voting, *both* proposals to cut rents were rejected and it was agreed to cut the rates instead. In other words, a proposal that was opposed by a majority of the council was accepted under a majority voting procedure. We have in this case a prime example of *politics as collective choice*. Diverse policy preferences have to be combined into a single decision. More importantly, we have an example of a *paradox of collective choice:* sometimes when preferences are combined the result is one which a majority dislikes, even though the process for combining these preferences involves the use of a majority voting rule.

THE PARADOX OF MAJORITY VOTING

Let us examine our example in more detail in order to understand what the study of politics as collective choice involves. On the district council each of the political parties voted as a group, so for the purposes of analysis we can treat them as three individuals. This is a great help, since the analysis of majority voting obviously requires at least three individuals. To be able to limit our analysis to three individuals means that we are dealing with the simplest and most straightforward case. Each individual political party has preferences over the alternatives that the council is faced with. More precisely, each individual party has a *preference ordering* over the alternatives. A preference ordering is simply a list of the alternatives ranked from most liked to least liked. For example, we know that the Conservatives preferred most a rates cut. If we also suppose that they preferred a weekly cut in rents to two free weeks, then we have their complete preference ordering: most liked is the rates cut; next liked is the cut in weekly rents; and least liked is a rent-free two weeks.

Now in order to understand how the majority of the council could end up with a result that they did not want, we have to construct the preference orderings for all the individual agents. This is the part of a collective-choice theory that involves art and skill rather than simple mechanical logic. In the present case there is a certain pattern of preference orderings that will enable us to understand our paradox. Suppose for each of the individuals we write the preferences from left to right in order from most liked to least liked, then we should have the pattern represented in table 3.1. Given that preference pattern, we can see how the council got into the tangle that it did. The order in which the alternatives are taken becomes important. Following normal committee procedure the amendment is voted on first against the original proposal. The winner from that vote goes on to the second vote against the *status quo.*

The Liberal amendment is voted on first against the Labour proposal for a weekly rent cut. Although the Liberals favour the proposal for two rent-free weeks, both the Labour and the Conservative groups prefer the weekly rent cut. So the amendment is lost and the main motion comes up against the policy of cutting the rates. Now only the Labour group supports the rent cut, since both the Liberals and the Conservatives prefer the proposal to cut the rates. The final result is that the decision is to cut the rates, although both Labour and the Liberals would prefer a rent cut. As the *status quo* point, the rate cut goes through without any further voting taking place.

TABLE 3.1   PATTERN OF PREFERENCE ORDERINGS

	First preference	Second preference	Third preference
Conservatives	Rate cut	Weekly rent cut	Two free weeks
Liberals	Two free weeks	Rate cut	Weekly rent cut
Labour	Weekly rent cut	Two free weeks	Rate cut

Notice something very important about the pattern of preferences in table 3.1. If the pattern were slightly different, the policy of the rate cut would not have succeeded. If Labour had been prepared to support the Liberal amendment, then the result would have been a rent cut, although this would have taken the form of two free weeks. Similarly, if the Liberals had been prepared to support Labour against the rate cut, then weekly rents could have been reduced. However, both parties have very strong tactical reasons for not supporting the position of the other. As rival opposition parties they want to distinguish their own position from that of the other in order to gain credibility with the electorate. The Liberals fear the voter who says 'If the Liberals vote with Labour, then I might as well vote Labour' and the Labour group fears the voter who says 'If Labour votes with the Liberals, then I might as well vote Liberal.' The result is that the Labour and Liberal majority on the council ends up with the policy which in combination it could overturn.

The pattern of preferences represented in table 3.1 can be described more formally and applied to other situations. If we label the individuals A, B and C and we label the alternatives x, y and z, then the pattern will be that contained in table 3.2. As we move from individual to individual each alternative is moved up one in the preference order of the second individual and the top alternative becomes the lowest. This pattern of preferences was first identified by the Marquis de Condorcet. (Condorcet was a leading aristocratic radical in the French Revolution, who was subsequently outlawed and condemned to death for his independence of mind by the revolutionary government.) This pattern will always lead to a situation in which any one alternative can always be beaten by a majority coalition. The example is known as Condorcet's paradox, and it is at the heart of most contemporary analyses of collective choice.

TABLE 3.2.   FORMAL PATTERN OF PREFERENCE ORDERINGS

	First preference	Second preference	Third preference
A	x	y	z
B	z	x	y
C	y	z	x

So far we have seen how an understanding of the preference orderings of political actors will help us understand an otherwise rather puzzling instance of political behaviour. Our approach has rested on identifying the following elements in the political situation we wanted to understand:

1 The individuals or political actors involved.
2 The set of alternatives for action that those individuals faced.
3 The preference orderings those individuals had over those alternatives.
4 The procedure, that is majority voting, by which those individual preferences were translated into a collective choice.

From these very simple elements we have begun to tell quite a complicated story of how one political outcome arose. But, you may ask, can we apply our understanding of Condorcet's paradox more generally?

We can apply our logic of collective choice to understand the problem of *political instability*. Clearly, a situation like the one in which a majority of a local council fails to get its way over rent cuts is highly unstable. The majority is not going to rest content for long with having its intentions frustrated in this way. In the real-life example the Labour and

Liberal groups were subsequently successful in passing a motion for a rent cut. In other real-life situations compromise of this sort is not always possible. Individuals stick by their original preference orderings. In these circumstances political instability is built into the collective-choice situation. Whoever currently occupies office faces the prospect of being ousted by the majority coalition that is latent in the opposition. Collective choice theorists have seen the increasingly frequent alternation of political parties in and out of office in liberal democracies as a symptom of there being divergent and incompatible preferences among the electorate.

Some people go even further than this observation, however. They believe that the existence of Condorcet's paradox undermines the intellectual justification for democracy. [1] They say that majority voting ought always to enable us to make a choice. Condorcet's paradox tells us that there are some preference patterns from which we are not able to choose by majority voting, or, what amounts to the same thing, if we can choose we do so only by stopping the voting at an arbitrary point. From this fact some people have concluded that the principle of majority rule has no claim on our allegiance. This is, however, rather a drastic conclusion to draw, and it is not clear that Condorcet's paradox does undermine the principle of democracy. Not all situations of majority voting involve a preference pattern of the Condorcet type. Where they do not, majority voting will yield an alternative that is favoured above all others by a majority of those voting. Moreover, work by collective-choice theorists has shown that there is no other method of voting which does not suffer the same weakness as majority rule. [2] Finally, when we have instances of Condorcet's paradox, it is not clear what the result ought to be, and so it is not clear that majority rule ought to yield a result. In order to appreciate this last point, consider the problem of what the result of the council's decision should have been, given the preferences represented in table 3.1 and a desire to reflect the balance of opinion among council members.

So far we have considered a very specific example, but the same logic can be applied wherever we have a set of actors, a set of alternatives, information on the preference ordering of the actors over the alternatives and a procedure for combining preferences into a collective choice. For example, we can apply the logic to an electorate choosing

[1]   Robert Paul Wolfe, *In Defense of Anarchism* (New York, 1970), pp. 58-67.
[2]   William H. Riker, *Liberalism Against Populism* (San Francisco, 1982).

among party candidates; to members of a legislature voting on laws; to members of a Cabinet deciding on policies; or to representatives of nation-states voting in an international body like the UN. We do not even need to restrict ourselves solely to formal situations. The informal choices of families or friends can exhibit the same logic. It is quite common among a group of friends deciding where to go for an evening meal to find a majority in favour of the Indian restaurant over the Chinese, a majority in favour of the Italian restaurant over the Indian, and a majority in favour of the Chinese restaurant over the Italian. In such cases a collective-choice problem exists, assuming the friends want to stay together for the evening, and an understanding of the preference patterns among the individuals involved will help us understand why some collective choices are so difficult to make.

The fact that we can use the same ideas and logic of collective choice to understand both party political voting and the informal choices of family or friends points towards a particular interpretation of politics and the way it can be studied. There are at least two approaches to the definition of politics. On the one hand, we can define it in terms of certain *institutions* in which human activity is conducted. In this approach politics is defined as what goes on in the state and its associated bodies. On the other hand, we can define politics as a *set of processes* that goes on within the whole range of human institutions. For the collective-choice theorists, these processes are those that are involved when a group of people has to adopt a common course of action. The need to make the common decision is what motivates the individuals involved to bargain, contract, vote or negotiate with one another.

There is no God-given way by which we can decide which of these two approaches is correct. In some circumstances, if only for the reason that time and human energies are limited, we may choose to concentrate our attention on the state and its associated bodies. In other circumstances, we find that the tools we bring to the study of family, workplace or sports club can be applied as well to local government, the state or international relations. If we find ourselves making what can sometimes be interesting and striking comparisons, why should we not explore them in detail?

In our opening example, we have looked at politics as a process of collective choice where there is a relatively formal mechanism, like voting, for combining individual preferences into a collective decision. In the next section we shall look at some other political processes in which there is no such formal mechanism. Once again the unexpected turns out to have an explanation in terms of actors, their preferences and the alternatives they face.

SELF-INTEREST, LARGE NUMBERS AND FREE RIDERS

Suppose there is a water shortage. It is in everyone's interest not to waste water. They can save water by washing their cars less frequently, not watering the lawn so often and not filling the baby's paddling pool. Yet experience suggests that people find it extremely difficult voluntarily to take conservation measures. During the water shortage of 1976 in Britain, for example, some water authorities had to put in standpipes or cut the water off at certain times of the day in order to ration available supplies of water. There is no doubt that these rationing devices are more onerous than voluntary conservation measures. Why should people fail to act in their own interest by not voluntarily conserving water when they had the opportunity to do so?

The answer, once again, is to be found in the pattern of individual preferences. Effective water conservation requires a large number of people voluntarily to limit their water use, but it does not require everyone to limit their water use. If everyone but you is conserving water, then you can carry on as before since your use is, literally, a drop in the ocean. No individual's contribution is significant. Consequently everyone can reason as follows. Either enough individuals will voluntarily save enough to make conservation effective, or they will not. Suppose they do: then I might as well carry on as before. Suppose they do not: then I still might as well carry on as before, since there is no advantage to me in making voluntary savings when no one else is doing so. In other words, each individual, quite rationally, has an incentive to 'free ride' on other people. But since everyone has this incentive the result is to undermine the collective effort. Individual rationality produces collective irrationality. (In other words, it sometimes pays to be stupid.)

It is worth stressing the nature of the individual rationality that is involved in this free-rider example. One crucial feature is that there is no advantage to an individual in saving water *whatever anyone else does*. Either enough other people are going to make the effort or they are not. Any one individual's contribution, taken on its own, is so small that it has no effect in determining whether enough people will make the effort. Any individual can control only his or her own actions. He or she cannot make sufficient other people take voluntary conservation measures to render that strategy effective. Therefore, from the individual's point of view, it is out of his or her control whether or not a sufficient number of individuals will take conservation measures.

The second crucial feature is that the benefits from voluntary conservation measures are collective. That is, everyone enjoys the benefits, for example by not having one's supply cut off at various times of the day, whether or not they have contributed personally to the voluntary saving. Everyone receives the benefit whether or not they have contributed to its existence by making voluntary savings themselves. If it were possible to restrict the benefits only to those who had made the voluntary saving, then there would be less of a problem. But in many situations, of which water supply is a clear example, it is not possible to make this restriction.

There are many situations in modern political life where large numbers of people are required to co-operate together in order to produce a benefit but where the benefit, once produced, cannot be restricted just to those who have co-operated in producing the benefit. Pollution control measures often have this characteristic. For health and other reasons it is in every householder's interest to have clean air free from pollution, but the cost to be borne is that every household has to burn more expensive smokeless fuel. In these circumstances everyone has an incentive to be part of the minority that gets away with burning less expensive untreated coal rather than more expensive smokeless fuel. But this of course is self-defeating for everyone involved. Similar reasoning applies to litter, the protection of parkland and open spaces, river and water pollution or traffic congestion and the decision that each individual has to make about the use of private or public transport.

The logic of the free rider operates most clearly when individuals have a strong economic incentive to avoid making their contribution to a collective benefit. So we can use the free rider analysis to understand the politics of economics. Let us consider three examples which illustrate the free-rider problem when individuals have an economic incentive to avoid making a contribution.

(1) Trade unions provide many collective benefits for their members. They negotiate wage and salary levels as well as conditions of service. They participate in the health and safety regulation of the workplace,

and they negotiate sickness and retirement benefits. Individual workers receive these benefits whether or not they belong to the union. Individuals therefore have an incentive to enjoy these benefits without paying a subscription to the union. The consequence of a large number of individuals doing this is, of course, to weaken the union's ability to provide these collective benefits. It is for this reason that many union activists press for the 'closed shop', the arrangement by which all of those who work in a place are required to belong to the union. This arrangement ensures that those who receive the collective benefits also pay their contribution towards their production.

(2) A further example of the free-rider problem occurs in what is sometimes referred to as 'the wages jungle'. In a modern economy the rate of increase in prices is in large measure dependent upon wages costs. If every group of workers is successful in negotiating a wage increase that is greater than any increase in productivity they can deliver, then the overall effect will be simply to raise the general level of prices, leaving each group of workers no better off in real terms than they were before. When everyone is standing on tiptoe, no one sees any better. Equally, however, if everyone else is standing on tiptoe then there is no advantage to any individual in staying on flat feet. So, if every union is negotiating inflationary wage increases, there is no advantage to any individual union in restraining its own wage demands. By implementing wage restraint on an individual basis, the union would merely be creating a situation in which its members faced price increases without having any compensating wage increases. The situation would be exactly the same as that of the private householder saving water in a drought when everyone else is using water freely. As one trade unionist once said of wage-bargaining in the labour market: 'In a free for all, we merely want to be part of the all.'

In thinking about the wages jungle many people have been led to advocate a statutory incomes policy, precisely because they see the problem as being one of controlling free riders. A statutory incomes policy changes the structure of incentives that faces any individual group of wages negotiators. By attaching legal penalties to wage increases above a given norm, the incentive to contribute to the collective benefit of orderly wages growth is given an individual form. The logic of the argument is the same as that which we noted in the case of the closed shop. The problem is not one which individuals can solve on their own. It needs a change in the pattern of incentives built into the situation.

(3) The third example we shall consider in the politics of economics concerns the ability of third-world countries to obtain higher prices for their commodities and raw materials. An obvious strategy among suppliers of any materials on the world market is to seek higher prices by an agreement among suppliers to restrict the amount that comes on to the market. If a commodity like coffee is restricted in supply then the market prices will rise and producers will obtain higher returns. For many commodities and raw materials a number of countries is responsible for supplying the world market. To restrict supply therefore involves a cartel arrangement or agreement among separate producers. However, if we look at the preferences of any individual producing country we can see once again how the free-rider problem arises. Any one country is tempted to take advantage of the restraint of the others, and release more of a commodity than agreed on to the world market in order to gain the advantage of higher prices. By acting in this way the individual country is hoping to capture both the collective benefits of the cartel arrangement and the individual benefit of a higher return on its sales. In this case, the basic motivation is not so much the small contribution which any individual's action makes to the overall market, but the discrepancy between collective benefit and individual contribution. Since every country has an incentive to act in the same way, the price will fall in response to all parties to the cartel trying to steal some advantage. Historically, cartel arrangements among third-world producers have been difficult to maintain for these reasons. Even if any agreement can be negotiated, the parties to that agreement have a strong incentive not to abide by its terms. Unlike the closed shop and wages jungle cases, it is difficult to see any central authority being in a position to change the structure of incentives that face individual actors. There is no international agency that could police a cartel arrangement and hence no obvious way of overcoming the free-rider problem. (Note, incidentally, that the successful OPEC cartel is not really a counter-example to the above, because it contains one producer, Saudi Arabia, whose volume of production by itself is sufficient to influence the world price on its own. Saudi Arabia by itself therefore can police the pricing policy.)

In thinking about these and other examples, collective-choice theorists have given much thought to the implications of the free-rider problem and the ways in which it might be overcome. One solution has already been mentioned in passing, namely the imposition by a central authority, under threat of penalty, of standards of behaviour that are consistent with the production of the collective benefit. However, this solution is not always available, and other possibilities have been canvassed. One attractive idea is to make co-operative behaviour the condition for receiving a selective individual benefit in addition to the collective benefit. For example, trade unions provide some benefits which are only available to their members: they represent members, and only members, before disciplinary tribunals and they negotiate discount schemes with local shops where the discount is only given on production of a union membership card. These selective benefits provide individuals with an incentive to join the union and so contribute via the membership fee to the collective benefit.

Another solution to the free-rider problem is moral education. Free riders are attempting to secure an advantage over other individuals without there being a special reason why they should have that advantage. Many people regard this sort of behaviour as unfair. If enough people can be educated to think that it would be unfair and unethical for them to free ride on the contribution of others, then their consciences will act as an internal incentive for them to maintain their contribution to the collective benefit. In practice, of course, contributions to collective benefits are maintained by a mixture of all three of these methods: political authority, selective economic incentives and moral education. The exact balance among these three will depend on various factors, for example the size of the group involved and the degree of identification among its members. Efforts at moral education are more likely to be effective in small, coherent groups than in large, varied ones. It is easier to imagine mounting an effective anti-litter campaign in a small village by means of moral education and the face-to-face disapproval of which villages are capable, than it is to imagine keeping together an international cartel of producers by means solely of moral education.

There are many situations in which the free-rider problem might arise, and it is something of an art to explain why it does not arise when we might expect it to. As a way of bringing out this point I shall conclude this section with an example, set as a puzzle to the reader. The puzzle is to explain in the example why the free-rider problem does not arise in a more acute form than it does.

From the point of view of any individual, the act of voting in modern, large-scale democracies would appear to be irrational. Even if you have strong preferences, distinguishing one political party from another, the chance that your individual vote will be decisive in getting that party elected means that the effective value of your vote is negligible. However, it is only because a large proportion of eligible citizens vote, that the democratic system is kept in being. Without the participation of those people the democratic system would wither. On the assumption that a democratic system is a collective benefit, we can regard those who vote as making a voluntary contribution to the collective benefit of democratic stability. (We can leave aside the cases of countries where voting is required by law, without affecting the argument.) However, this would seem to be a case where we would expect the free-rider motive to operate. No individual's act of voting makes a significant difference to the aggregate level of turnout, and, if there is a sufficient turnout to maintain the democratic system, then everyone benefits whether or not they have personally voted. We seem then to have the makings of a situation in which we would expect the free-rider motive to operate. The puzzle, which is left to the reader, is: why do so many people vote?

PRISONERS OF THE ARMS RACE

In the previous section we looked at examples of collective choice where the preferences of the individuals involved depended usually upon the behaviour of large numbers of other individuals. We saw that, because no one individual could control the behaviour of all the other individuals, each person had an incentive to free ride upon the contribution of everyone else. It seems sensible to ask the following question: suppose we consider situations in which only a few individual agents are involved, do we find that individual preferences still run contrary to self-interest? As we shall see, the answer is that individual preferences may still run contrary to self-interest, even when two individual agents are involved.

In order to illustrate this point, consider the arms race. Effectively this is a contest between the USSR and the USA, and so we can look on it as a case of two-person conflict. We find in this example that the preferences of the individual agents are interdependent. This means that both are locked in a situation from which it is extremely difficult to escape, even though both would be better off if they did escape.

Let us look at the arms race from the point of view of first one protagonist and then the other. Consider first the situation from the point of view of the USSR. From the Soviet point of view it is better to have mutual nuclear disarmament than to have the arms race. However, it is worse to have the USA with nuclear weapons and the USSR without than to have the arms race. Conversely, it is better to have the USSR with nuclear weapons and the USA without than it is to have mutual disarmament. Writing down these preferences for Soviet policy makers, then, we have the following:

First preference	Second preference	Third preference	Fourth preference
USSR nuclear, USA disarmed	Both disarmed	Both nuclear	USA nuclear, USSR disarmed

In other words, the USSR would prefer the advantage, but if it cannot have that, then it would prefer mutual nuclear disarmament. From the point of view of the USA the preference pattern the situation is the same, except now of course the preference is for the USA to have the advantage; thus

First preference	Second preference	Third preference	Fourth preference
USA nuclear, USSR disarmed	Both disarmed	Both nuclear	USSR nuclear, USA disarmed

If you inspect these preference orderings, you will see that both the USSR and the USA prefer mutual disarmament to the arms race. Since it is clearly impossible for both to steal the advantage on one another, we might think that it would be easy for them both to agree to disarm mutually rather than continuing the arms race. But the arms race has now been going on for more than thirty years, so there must be some explanation of why the two sides fail to reach a mutually advantageous arrangement. To understand this explanation, we need to look at the preference patterns involved, and in particular we need to look at the way in which preferences are interdependent. Figure 3.1 represents this pattern of interdependence. Along the rows we represent the choice of the USSR and down the columns we represent the choice of the USA.

The cell entries record the four outcomes from the two possible choices.

FIGURE 3.1
THE PATTERN OF INTERDEPENDENCE IN THE ARMS RACE

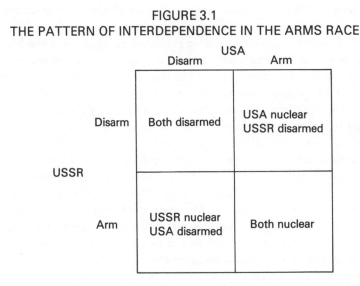

Now look again at the problem from the point of view of the USSR. It is confronted with the choice of arming or disarming, knowing that the USA is confronted with the same choice. Soviet decision-makers can reason as follows. Either the USA will disarm or it will not. Suppose the USA disarms. When we consult the preferences of the USSR we can see that in these circumstances the USSR would prefer to arm. Suppose the USA arms. Again, when we consult the preferences of the USSR, we can see that it would prefer to arm. So the best response of the USSR is to arm. Of course decision-makers for the USA can use exactly the same pattern of reasoning to show that whatever the USSR does it is always better for the USA to arm. The result is that both nations arm, *even though they would both prefer mutual disarmament.*

The situation is, of course, even worse than this simplified example shows. Both sides know that they are in this mutual disarmament dilemma, and both sides know that the other side is in the same dilemma. Hence both sides know that the other has a reason to arm, whatever it does itself. In real life this pressure towards the arms race shows up in the rhetoric that both sides use to justify their arms build-up: if the other side is arming, then the excuse is the need to respond;

if the other side pauses, then the excuse is the need to restore historic parity (read: advantage for our side).

This dilemma of interdependent decision-making is known as the Prisoners' Dilemma, after the original example which involved two prisoners having to decide whether or not to confess to a crime.[3] There are, however, a number of other situations in which the same logic applies. One such example is the difficulty which the USSR and Japan have in reaching agreement on limiting whale fishing. Both would prefer a situation of mutual limitation, but equally both would prefer even more a situation in which they had no limit on their whale fishing and the other side was restricted in its catch to a fixed quota. Another example, of quite a different sort, is the ideological battle between left and right in the British Labour Party. Both sides agree that it is better to have agreement than to have public warfare over the party's ideological position, but neither side can allow a situation in which the other might gain the advantage. Hence the warfare continues, even though both sides would prefer peace. And a final example is provided by the battle for TV ratings in Britain between independent television and the BBC. Both sides may agree that it is better to have rational programming, so that major sporting or entertainments features do not clash, but neither will withdraw its most attractive programmes from the key slots in case the other gains an advantage in consequence. Of course, both end up worse off in the long term, since viewers have an incentive to buy video-recorder equipment, to cover both sets of programmes, thus denying both independent television and the BBC a potential audience at other times.

Various ways out of the sorts of dilemmas outlined here have been explored by collective-choice theorists. One solution is similar to that suggested by the free-rider problem, namely to have some superior political authority impose a set of incentives that work towards the co-operative solution by penalizing non-cooperation. However, this

---

[3]   The 'prisoners' dilemma' originates in the following example. Two suspects are taken into custody by the police and separated. They are each told that the police suspect them of having committed a major burglary together. Each is told that if they both confess to the crime, then the police will recommend a lenient sentence. If neither confesses, then the police will prosecute them both on a minor charge where the evidence is watertight. However, if one of them confesses and the other does not, the confessor will be treated very lightly, but the non-confessor will have 'the book' thrown at him. The problem for each prisoner is whether to confess or not. The preferred outcome for each prisoner is (1) I confess, the other stays silent; (2) neither confesses; (3) both confess; (4) I stay silent, the other confesses. As can be seen, this is exactly the same structure of preferences as that discussed in the text in the case of the mutual disarmament dilemma.

solution faces the practical objection that arriving at an agreement to set up such a superior political authority is itself a form of Prisoners' Dilemma.

An alternative, and in some ways more promising, approach is to recognize that circumstances like those which create the arms race do not involve decisions taken at one point in time, but instead involve a sequence of decisions taken over time. It has been shown that co-operative action will more easily arise over time than in the one-off case, because one of the parties can take the initiative in co-operating knowing that it can 'punish' subsequent defection by the other side by adopting in later decisions a non-cooperative strategy.[4] Although the logic of this sort of mutual decision-making over time is now quite well understood, there is little research done on the social and psychological conditions that help create its emergence. We all know that the strategy 'I'll co-operate if you will – and, if not, I'll be a bloody nuisance' sometimes works extremely well. But we have little detailed understanding of why and when it works well. Until we do, we cannot pretend to have a theory of politics.

CONCLUSION

In the previous sections we have looked at three very different types of collective-choice problem. However, they have all had certain features in common. All have involved situations in which action according to self-interest led to undesirable outcomes, even from the viewpoint of the self-interested. In each case we have tried to understand this paradoxical result in terms of the preferences of individuals over the alternatives they face and the way these preferences are combined into a collective choice. What each of the examples has shown is that apparently prudent and sensible decisions lead to undesirable outcomes for those involved. Can anyone deny that these examples have a message for those who study politics in the twentieth century?

Michael Taylor, *Anarchy and Cooperation* (New York and London, 1976).

4

Politics: people, resources and power

ADRIAN LEFTWICH

1

When people think of 'politics' it is commonly the case that they identify it with a more or less exclusive 'public' realm of generally unpleasant squabbles and struggles for office and power – which may be violent in some circumstances. This is conventionally associated with the activities of political parties, pressure groups, revolutionary movements, elections, parliaments, congresses, military regimes, civil governments and the like. The way in which the mass media generally treat politics only serves to encourage such a view. The personalization of politics – 'Prime Minister attacks Opposition Leader', or 'Bitter fight in Shadow Cabinet', or 'New chief of Coal Board to be opposed by the unions' – has the systematic effect of trivializing its substance, and acts to confine our conceptions of politics to a generally very narrow band of usually formal institutions of government and state. Professional politicians (and officials of one kind and another) in their public statements, interviews and bickering do little to alter such conceptions of politics.

While the academic discipline of Politics tends in general to focus on the narrowly 'political' institutions of government in a manner that may be more analytical, it nonetheless leaves out *most* collective human activities *within* modern states as well as in historical and contemporary non-state societies. The sharp divisions of labour in the social sciences have caused such matters to be consigned to disciplines such as Economics, Sociology, Anthropology and History. And it certainly seems as if the consequence, if not the function, of this academic specialization serves actually to obscure understanding of our societies and their problems, not to enhance it.

The major purpose of this chapter is to challenge such narrow conventional conceptions of the character and scope of politics, to offer a much more inclusive definition of it, and to provide a preliminary framework of analysis for studying politics so defined. At the core of the argument will be the assertion that politics is at the heart of *all* collective social activity, formal and informal, public and private, in *all* human groups, institutions and societies, not just some of them, and that it always has been and always will be.[1] This view of politics enables us to incorporate into its study a far wider and richer range of social activities, past and present, than is normally the case in most teaching and research. Given this approach, it will be argued that politics is therefore to be found, for instance, in families, groups of kin or 'tribes', so called; in villages, towns, regions, nation-states and – in the modern world – on a global basis between them. Politics is also found in all formal institutions – such as churches, factories, bureaucracies, universities and clubs; as well as in political parties, trades unions, insurance offices, women's groups, chambers of commerce, parents' associations, *mafia* and armies, and in all the relations which may obtain between them. It is found too in more informal or even temporary groupings of people, in both modern and historical societies, in complex industrial societies or in structurally more simple and smaller subsistence-based or agrarian societies of all kinds, where there may be no formal institutions of government. Informal groups might include bus queues, football crowds, people meeting for the first time on a camp site, *ad hoc* pressure groups or voluntary associations; we might find them among children inventing and playing games; in collaborative working groups (for instance in many agrarian third-world societies today where people pool their labour and time to clear fields for cultivation and for harvesting); among the residents of a housing estate; or among ethnic communities of new migrants in the slums and shanty towns of the sprawling cities of Latin America, Africa and Asia.

Now it is certainly the case that there are obvious differences in their contexts, forms and particulars between the politics of a family or a school playground or an ethnic association of migrant workers, and those of national elections, revolutionary struggles or international

---

[1] For a fairly limited conception of politics, which is nonetheless coherent in its own terms, see Bernard Crick, *In Defence of Politics* (London, 1962; 3rd ed, 1982).

disputes. It is equally true that there are differences (for instance in respect of scope, scale and complexity) between the politics of a parish council, housing association or local tennis club on the one hand, and those of a modern government, multinational corporation or international official agency (like the World Bank) on the other hand. But, despite these differences, it is central to the argument here that all the activities which go on within or between such groups, institutions or societies involve politics. This chapter will seek to identify the common factors in all such instances which make such a claim reasonable, and will provide an introductory analytic framework in terms of which one may study any such collectivity.

It will also be argued here that most urgent problems (such as many epidemics, unemployment, crime, poverty and famine) which crop up in societies are in large part a product of our *politics*. They are *not* simply the result of 'human nature', natural disasters, acts of God or random and inexplicable eruptions in the open plane of human affairs, now here, now there. Nor can such problems be understood or explained only in terms of the usual technical or specialist interpretations offered, for instance, from within such disciplines as Medicine or Economics. They need to be explained *politically*, and this requires a wholeheartedly interdisciplinary approach.

It follows from this view that the study of politics, as defined here, should be the focal point and integrating purpose of the historical and social sciences, as well as all other disciplines (or branches within them) which have the condition and welfare of human beings in society as their primary concern. The wider the range of groups, institutions, societies and problems we are able to analyse, compare and understand politically, the more progress we shall make towards establishing an interdisciplinary and explanatory political science of society.

Such a broad conception, plus the comparative and historical claims entailed in it, rests on a particular definition of politics in human societies.[2] So, what is politics?

2

Politics is *not* a separate realm of public life and activity. On the contrary, politics comprises all the activities of co-operation and

[2] I have defined and elaborated the conception of politics used here at much greater length in Adrian Leftwich, *Redefining Politics: People, Resources and Power* (London, 1983).

conflict, within and between societies, whereby the human species goes about organizing the use, production and distribution of human, natural and other *resources* in the course of the production and reproduction of its biological and social life. These activities are nowhere isolated from other features of life in society, private or public. They everywhere both influence *and* reflect the distribution of power and patterns of decision-making, the structure of social organization, and the systems of culture and ideology in society or groups within it. And all this may further influence and reflect the relations of a society (or a group or institution within one) with both its natural environment and with other societies (or groups and institutions within them). This brief definition of politics requires some clarification and elaboration.

3

The first point to make is that the term 'resources' means, in broad terms, any things, both material and non-material, that people *use* to further their own ends, as individuals or collectively in groups. It includes the obvious material ones such as land, animals, income, capital and other natural resources such as rivers, forests, minerals and seas. But the term also denotes things which are non-material and which are not immediately thought of as 'resources', such as time, education, status, influence, opportunity and knowledge. It also, crucially, includes people – and not only in the limited sense of individuals as units of labour, but also as husbands, wives, children, grandparents and so on. In societies which are less familiar to people in the industrial societies of the north, the relations between such persons can be very important, not only in the social sense as we understand it, but in relation to productive activities.[3] It is also important to say that in the last twenty years, especially, the feminist movement has drawn sharp attention to the much ignored question of the role and contribution of women in the productive life of the societies of the north, and to the sexual division of labour associated with this. This is a whole area which has been largely excluded from the study of politics, but no longer can or should be.

Secondly, a central point to stress is that wherever the human species is (or has been) found, it is found living and working in groups which

[3] See, for instance, Barbara Rogers, *The Domestication of Women* (London, 1980).

we refer to simply as societies. These in turn are everywhere composed of a variety of (usually) smaller groups, formal or informal, which sometimes overlap or coincide with each other in their composition, and sometimes do not. These include familial, residential, educational, peer, religious, gender, recreational, productive, distributive and many other groups. For present purposes it is important to emphazise this *social* character of our existence as a species, and also that the activity of politics is inextricably bound up with it. For without social groupings there is no society and no politics: and without politics there can be no organized collective activities such as those mentioned above.

Now while our history as a species has involved our *physical* evolution over some three million years or more, from *homo habilis* to the emergence of *homo sapiens sapiens* at least 50,000 years ago, it is equally important to recognize that our development as a distinctive animal species has gone hand in hand with our *social* evolution.[4] For most of this history, as a species, human groups lived and worked by hunting and gathering in a variety of ways in an increasing number of places, and this activity continues today in some parts of the world, such as the Kalahari desert and the Amazon jungle. Then, from about 10,000 years ago, small groups of people first started to tend crops and domesticate animals in various places – the so-called 'neolithic revolution'. From this time onwards there has been a remarkable proliferation of different types of societies, organized around distinctive productive patterns, using, producing and distributing resources in diverse ways. Some have remained primarily agricultural, others pastoral, and yet others mixed. Some have come to rely on trade and commerce, or mining or industry, or a mixture of these in conjunction with various forms of agriculture. All have undergone change, and continue to do so, and not only in strictly productive terms. Around their productive systems great empires rose and fell. They include those of Ghana, Mali and Songhai in West Africa, before the sixteenth century; the Incas and Aztecs in pre-Columbian America; and those powerful Asian states and empires, for instance in India, Indo-China and China, long before European commercial and industrial development or imperial expansion. The great formal empires of the British, French, Dutch and Portuguese have also all but gone. And in the course of this long history of the human

[4] One can do no better than look at the following books for good introductory accounts of human social evolution. Andrew Sherratt (ed.), *The Cambridge Encyclopedia of Archaeology* (Cambridge, 1980); and Richard Leakey, *The Making of Mankind* (London, 1981).

species and the societies we have lived in, population has grown from an estimated ten million in 8000 BC to about 300 million at the time of Christ to the present figure of some 4000 million in 1983.

Thirdly, and most important for the argument, a central feature of the social life of the species is that we are *producers*, quite unlike any other animals. At the very heart of our social existence in groups is – and always has been – a very wide range of conscious and planned productive activities, involving the purposive use and production of resources. In the course of our long history – that is in the changing forms of our politics – the human species has come to use both old and new resources in different ways. Moreover, major technological innovations (a very specific form of resource use) have been achieved. These range from stone and then iron tool-kits and (vitally) fire on the one hand, through to computerized manufacturing processes and nuclear energy on the other hand. Around such diverse productive systems and their associated technologies, the rich mosaic of societies mentioned earlier has developed.

Prior to the fifteenth century, contact between these societies was generally local or regional, as was borrowing and the diffusion of ideas and techniques. But since the expansion of Europe from that time, and the establishment of the first transcontinental companies and empires, and then the modern transnational corporations, there are few societies today which are not more or less open to contact with each other. As a result of this, the resources of the world – such as capital, labour, technology and raw materials – are now increasingly used in productive processes on a global basis. [5]

Fourthly, these productive activities everywhere both required and increasingly involved the organization (either voluntarily or by force) of co-operation (literally, co-work) and communication within groups and then between them. Bands of hunter-gatherers, for instance, co-operated in subsistence production. People working in groups could more easily fell trees and place them across gullies or streams; nets could be more effectively used where and if organized hunting parties could flush game or fish into them. Among pastoral peoples, herds of animals could be gathered together and tended in large numbers. In agricultural societies, co-operative labour groups enabled tracts of land to be cleared, crops to be sown and harvests brought in. Among the so-called 'hydraulic' societies of south and south-east Asia, for instance, such

[5] See, for instance, Immanuel Wallerstein, *The Capitalist World Economy* (Cambridge, 1979).

highly organized productive work enabled remarkable irrigation systems to be devised, built and maintained. Elsewhere, larger and larger ships could be built and sailed further, roads constructed, coal mined on an intensive scale, factories set up and operated, and so forth. The global character of much modern production, as mentioned earlier, can be illustrated by considering a typical pair of running or tennis shoes. The raw materials (like rubber) may come from Malaysia, the finance capital from a consortium of European banks, the technology from a machine designed and built in America, while the labour and the factory may be in Taiwan, South Korea or the Repulic of Ireland, for instance. In different combinations and in different places, the same is often true today for cars, television sets, watches and furniture.[6]

In short, all productive activities – from the most local and technologically simple to the global and most complex – have involved various forms of purposive and organized co-operation between human beings, living and working in groups. And changes in the way communities have used and produced resources have been at the core of changes in their politics, whether these have had internal or external origins, or whether they have come about through innovation or force.

These productive and distributive activities are at the core of all politics. But around and in the course of all this, in every human society, a variety of other social and cultural activities and skills emerged – such as rituals, ceremonies, art, music, games and of course language. These, too, either required or enhanced co-operation and communication, and further facilitated innovation, adaptation and borrowing. All acted to sustain and to elaborate patterns of social life.

When you look even casually at any society today or in the past it quickly becomes apparent just how many group productive and social activities there are or have been in them. Some are strictly productive – such as hunting, farming, manufacturing, mining, building and so on. Others are more obviously cultural, ceremonial or ritual. These latter might include, for instance, dancing round a camp-fire among the !Kung San of the Kalahari desert, or in the village hall or disco in modern Britain; story-telling or dancing to gong music in an Iban longhouse in Sarawak, or the production of a play in a school or theatre in New York; or burial activities and ceremonies, which may involve placing the dead under cairns of stones, or exposing dismembered bodies

[6] Nigel Harris, *Of Bread and Guns* (London, 1983), chs 4 and 5.

to the elements, or incineration at crematoria. All the social and cultural activities within all societies which are associated with birth and marriage are further examples of this.

Of course, some activities may be simultaneously productive and also cultural, ritual or ceremonial. Thus, for instance, pastoralists living in the more arid regions of East Africa may have more or less complex and regular rain-making ceremonies, and they may sing to and about their cattle. In such and other societies in Africa the transfer of cattle between families at marriage has great significance in both productive and social terms. In the Midwest of the USA or in rural South Africa and Australia one finds churches organizing special services, in times of drought, in which prayers are offered for rain.

Then there is the vast range of other collective human activities which do not fall easily into either the strictly 'productive' or 'social' categories, but which involve people working in groups for or against some particular use or distribution of resources. A local pressure group on a housing estate which is demanding the establishment of a crèche or a proper pedestrian crossing by the local authority could be a typical example. Elsewhere, people campaigning against the routing of a new trunk road in a particular vicinity, or in favour of better transport facilities for old-aged pensioners or the disabled, would be other examples.

Wherever one finds human groups, one finds such collective activities: all of them, productive or social, in some way involve activities concerned with organizing the use, production or distribution of resources. That's politics.

Finally, it should be clear that such activities do not only involve co-operation, but regularly entail conflict, sometimes mild and sometimes violent, within or between groups, institutions and societies. This is true whatever grouping of people, formal or informal, large or small, one may focus on for analytical purposes, whether it be a band of hunter-gatherers or a complex industrial society; whether it be a family or group of kin, a club, office, school, trade union, board of directors, multinational corporation, political party or government agency – or in any of the relations which may occur between them. And it is systematically the case that such conflicts have to do with the use, production and especially the distribution of resources, or with attempts to change or defend ways in which this happens. And that's politics.

The discussion thus far should have helped to clarify the conception of politics being advanced here and to have provided some preliminary indication of its scope and applicability. At the heart of the approach is the claim that wherever we live and work in groups, and whatever we do in our collective productive and social lives, we are always engaged in activities of co-operation and conflict over the use, production and distribution of resources. That is, we are constantly engaged in politics.

That most of these activities are usually thought of or defined as 'non-political' or beyond politics, seems rather arbitrary. For in principle they are no different to the larger (sometimes) national activities of co-operation and conflict which occur within or around the formal institutional and 'public' realm, associated usually with government and the state. These may be between competing elites, classes or parties, seeking power to direct the main lines of policy about the national use and distribution of resources — be these to do with production in nationalized or private industries, defence or welfare service expenditures, or taxes and social security provisions and so forth. Moreover, there have been many (and still are some) societies in human history which have not had formally separate institutional realms of government, and it seems both odd and limiting to have to conclude that they therefore have or have had no politics.

In short, then, in all societies at all levels and in all human groups and institutions within them — from family and kin groups to the state, and from tennis clubs to multinational corporations — there is politics.

But how, in any given instance, can one go about analysing the politics of any one of these in order to compare it with others? What, in other words, are the analytical and comparative implications of this view of politics?

4

In answering this question I shall suggest a series of *related* analytical starting points which flow directly from the definition of politics given earlier. Each of these concentrates on one of the five main features which are always found and are more or less clearly identifiable in *any* collectivity of people, formal or informal, private or public, temporary or established, static or changing.

These are, first, its typical principles and activities of resource use and distribution; secondly, its structure of power and decision-making;

thirdly, its system of social organization; and fourthly and fifthly, the central elements of its culture and ideology. It is very important at the outset to stress that these features are *not* separate or independent spheres of life in a society, institution or group. In practice they are inextricably related activities, behaviours, relationships and outlooks which – taken together – compose the defining characteristics of any collectivity of people and hence constitute its politics. But one can start by discussing them in turn.

For a society as a whole the first things to establish, therefore, are the central principles and processes which govern the ownership, control and use of the major productive resources – such as land, water, animals, capital, tools, factories etc. For instance, what is the balance between, say, private (individual, familial, corporate) and public (that is, communal or state) ownership and control? What is the pattern of their distribution within the population? Is it even or uneven, say between regions, classes, religious or ethnic groups? And what are the principles and practices governing the distribution not only of such resources, but the products and rewards of work associated with their usage (say in the form of food, shelter or income)? Is the free market left to organize distribution? Or does the state do it, for instance through detailed planning and rationing? Or is distribution left to smaller communal groupings (families, groups of kin, villages, etc)? Or is it some combination of these? In the course of this work is a surplus produced over and above immediate needs, and what happens to it? Is it stored for later consumption, or exchanged or invested, and by whom? How much of what people produce do they keep for themselves and how much flows 'outwards' and 'upwards', say in the form of tribute, tithes or taxes? And to whom? How much of that in turn flows 'inwards' and 'downwards' to the community, and in what form? Does it get redistributed, for instance, in the form of public roads, educational and health services, protection or insurance against lean times? And is this, in turn, evenly distributed between social groups or regions?

For a smaller group or institution within a society the same kinds of question must first be asked. What resources does it have at its disposal, and where do they come from? In a family, for instance, this may include the contributions from the earnings of its members, plus state grants, and perhaps inheritances from relatives. But family resources also include the house (rented or being bought on a mortgage), the members of the family, plus all the possessions and equipment (such as cars and bikes) they may have. For a factory, the resources will include of course the fixed capital of buildings and machinery, the raw materials which are processed, the labour, plus the capital paid up by shareholders as well as bank loans, and earnings from sales. In a club, the resources may consist of the club-house and greens, funds from subscriptions, loans and other functions, plus the membership itself. In a typical British university the main financial resources will consist of a grant from the government administered through the University Grants Committee (UGC), plus the fees (paid privately or by local authorities) as well as the buildings, equipment and so forth. But there are also the staff, students and additional resources which come through research grants, for instance.

In such groups and institutions, just as in a society as a whole, it is important to identify the patterns of resource ownership or control, use and distribution, for the real core of their politics has to do with all the activities of co-operation and conflict that will be involved in this.

But it was argued earlier that all these activities of politics, and their outcome over time, in any collectivity, both influence *and* reflect its distribution of power and patterns of decision-making, as well as its structure of social organization and its systems of culture and ideology. This needs to be explained and illustrated before exploring the way in which all these elements relate and interrelate in the politics of specific examples.

Secondly, then, one needs to analyse the structure of power and decision-making which directly influences how decisions are made, for any collectivity, especially about the central matters of production and distribution. For in a society, as well as in groups and institutions within one, power is generally closely related to the ownership or control of resources. Whatever may be the focus of analysis, power may be found to be concentrated in a few hands or more or less widely distributed. There may be a number of decision-making groups, and these may be family heads, age-sets, village leaders, chiefs, committees (or a hierarchy of them), elected or appointed representatives, landlords, boards of directors, public officials, members of parliament or congress, cabinets, civil servants, presidents or monarchs, etc., or some combination of them. Do these decision-making centres of power overlap, co-operate or conflict, and over what and why? Is there wide consultation or are there strict lines of command and authority? Do some people (social, sexual or ethnic groups, a certain class, males or particular clans, for instance) regularly have more power or more frequent access to it? If so, why? Is there any connection between birth and power, ownership and power, class and power, wealth and power, sex and power or achievement and power? In seeking to analyse the politics of any group, institution or society one must become clear about this, whether one is looking at a family, a club, a university, a factory, a government, an international private or public agency, or a society as a whole. For the structure of power and decision-making – and its basis – is clearly important in determining how resources get used and distributed. However, it is very important *not* to assume – as is often done – that an understanding of this is sufficient for an understanding of politics in any collectivity: it is not. For although it is important, it is only one of the five main features outlined earlier. For while power is a resource in its own right, it is necessary also to explain its distribution and also how and why it is used in some ways and not others in any given instance. I have already suggested how closely the sources of power are usually related to the ownership and control of other resources, and hence why an understanding of the *relations* between ownership, control and power is so crucial in the analysis of politics. But there are other factors which help to shape and yet also reflect the distribution of power and the character of decision-making processes, and hence the politics of any particular case. And it is thus important to turn to look at these now.

Thus, thirdly, every collectivity, formal or informal, has a system of social organization, which is closely bound up with the patterns of ownership and control of resources and hence also the structure of power. 'Social organization' refers to the formal or informal structuring *and* relations of groups within a society or institution. Thus societies as wholes may have major divisions within them, along lines of caste, class, ethnicity, colour or culture, for instance. Smaller communities within societies may be organized socially into lineages, clans, age-sets, 'tribes' or regions. Within or between any of these, marriage may be endogamous or exogamous, and families may be typically nuclear or extended, monogamous or polygamous, matriarchal or patriarchal in their social organization. Institutions, too, have systems of social organization, and universities offer illustrations of this. Their social organization may be composed of social and power hierarchies of professors, readers, senior lecturers, lecturers, secretarial and technical staff, plus cohorts of students in different years and departments. All of this corresponds not only with a particular division of labour and specialization, but usually also with distinctive statuses, rights, powers and responsibilities. Different universities may have different forms of organization within and between departments. There may be sharp distinctions between where people eat in them (Junior Common Rooms, refectories, staff canteens and Senior Common Rooms), the kinds of offices and rooms they have, and the manner in which different groups are characteristically addressed and dressed. Such factors of social organization are important in the politics of any institution — whether it be a factory, bureaucracy or church. They help to define and also express the contours along which both co-operation and conflict may flow. In some societies, to take it further, relations by blood or marriage, or membership of particular clans or castes, may have very important implications for an individual's position in the productive, social or power structures of the society. In others, membership of certain classes, parties, clubs, organizations (or the school one attended) may be more important. Thus social organization may decisively influence the life chances of individuals and groups, and hence the politics of a society more generally.

Finally, to take the fourth and fifth features together, all societies, institutions and groups have at least one system of culture and ideology, and sometimes more than one. Culture here means a more or less wide network of standardized customs and regular behaviours — or ways of doing things. It includes typical customs of courtship, marriage and socialization of the young; the basic styles of dress; food habits and taboos; principles of hospitality, and much more. These differ in their forms and particulars from society to society, and often between different sections (for instance classes and religious groups) within them. All institutions, too, have cultures. Universities, for instance, may be said to have certain academic cultures: that is, their preferred and standard ways of doing things like teaching, learning and examining, plus all their rituals, ceremonies and procedures. So too do clubs, factories, churches and voluntary associations, as a moment's thought will indicate. So too do families.

Ideology refers to such things as religious beliefs and practices, myths, values, moral codes and norms; that is, the general ideas and attitudes which serve to endorse certain forms of behaviour and frown on others. And, for present purposes, it includes artistic activities and forms, and the status and kind of scientific knowledge. But it also refers more broadly to the outlooks ('lenses', so to speak) in terms of which people in particular collectivities (perhaps societies as wholes, or cultures or classes within them) interpret the world about them. In some societies and institutions (say modern Britain or a typical commercial organization) it may be thought both good and proper for people to compete actively with each other for advancement, wealth and success. In others (say the !Kung San of the Kalahari or a community of priests or nuns) co-operation and self-denial may be thought a better way of behaving. And it is important to recognize that ideologies, in either the broad or narrow sense, are not simply free-floating and abstract bodies of ideas and beliefs which have no other significance. They have very direct implications for behaviour and the use and distribution of resources.

Thus, cultures and ideologies are bound up in the politics of any group, and cultural conflicts between groups constitute part of the politics of some societies. Cultures and ideologies form part of the broadly common 'language' of shared behaviours, meanings and understandings which make interaction possible within a group or society. They both embody and help to shape the ways in which resources (human and other) are used and distributed. And, in the final analysis, conflicts between cultures and ideologies in societies turn out to be conflicts between different ways of doing things, or of wanting things to be done; that is, different ways of resource use and distribution, whether this be to do with strictly material or non-material resources. As illustration one can point to disputes over the eating or non-eating of pork; or the insistence on the subservience or equality of women; or the observance or non-observance of the sabbath for purposes of commercial activity. In larger terms, the conflict between 'socialism' and 'capitalism' is much more than simply the conflict of 'ideologies'. In short, what are often thought to be only 'moral' or ideological disputes (which of course they also are) have very important implications of a much more practical and material kind. For these and other reasons it is necessary to understand the culture/s and ideology/ies of the collectivity one is studying, in order to comprehend its politics.

5

This related set of five main analytical starting points — for short-hand purposes I call it the analytical framework from here on — can be used with considerable effect for explaining the politics of *any* human group, institution or society, though it is not always straightforward. In a large society or institution, for example, the evidence may not be easy to obtain or assemble in the way one wishes to. And in a small-scale society or institution, or informal grouping, it is not always a simple matter to discern the character of the elements discussed in the previous section, or the relations between them. Nonetheless, it has been done and can be done. So before concluding this chapter it will be useful to give some illustrations of how one might proceed, whatever the collectivity that is of interest to one. I use some of the examples which have been scattered, without much exploration thus far, in the previous pages.

Given the definition used here, there is clearly politics in the family in all societies, though this of course differs in broad terms between societies (and often between particular social groups within them) as well as in the micro-details of specific families. Nonetheless, an application of the main features of the analytical framework to families can yield some interesting diagnoses of their politics.

All families are engaged in activities involving co-operation and conflict over the use, production and distribution of resources, and so it is important to establish what these are in any instance. The resources at issue of course will include food, space, time, income, opportunities, labour — to mention but a few. In some families decisions may have to be made between different possible uses of such resources — such as going on holiday or redecorating the kitchen; or between new clothes for the children or a new carpet in the hall; or who is to mow the lawn, clean the house and the car, or wash the dishes, and so on. Are the latter tasks done by rota? Or do the males do some of them (cleaning the car, mowing the lawn), while the females do others (cook and clean the house)? Is the division of labour sexual, and is there agreement about this, and why? There may be disputes over the distribution of food or income (for instance in relation to housekeeping or pocket money). Elsewhere, in many third-world societies, for instance, family resources (notably labour) have to be organized for preparing the fields, sowing and harvesting the crops, tending the cattle and milking the cows. In polygamous families, in many parts of Africa, for instance, tensions may arise amongst wives, or between them and their husbands, over unequal or improper treatment – perhaps with regard to the location of their huts, or their plots of land or domestic property. And in India, where development agencies have helped and encouraged women to become involved in village-level craft production, conflict may arise over whether they or their husbands control the income they receive from their work.

In exploring further the politics of families in this way it next becomes necessary to analyse the structure of power and decision-making about such matters, and here too the social organization, culture and ideology of the family – and more broadly in the society as a whole – will be influential. Is decision-making left entirely to the male head of the family, as is the characteristic pattern in strongly patriarchal societies? Or do husband and wife tend to consult and take decisions jointly? Or are some matters (clothes, food, cooking, many domestic items?) decided by the wife, and others (domestic machinery, choice of car?) decided by the husband? If male power is dominant, are there any external constraints on this? In some societies the influence of the wife's family (or her brother, in some instances) may be much greater than in others. In such and other societies (and again there are good examples from Africa) marriage is not simply a union of two people, but of two families, and this involves a complex of mutual duties, rights, obligations and responsibilities, which may be enforced by the families. These are practices which are less commonly found and are certainly less strong in the much more privatized 'nuclear' families of the industrial and urban societies, where the internal politics of the family tend to be more autonomous, and where 'in-laws' are not thanked for 'interfering'. Unlike the pattern in the north, the family in many societies of the third world (and especially its rural areas) is not nuclear, but 'extended'. It is often composed not only of the husband and wife, but also grandparents, unmarried adult offspring as well as sometimes unmarried brothers or sisters. This generally larger family and its social organization has far-reaching implications for resource use and distribution.

Moreover, the culture and ideology of a society (or of specific social groups and families within it) will in other ways influence the resource use and division of labour, and reflect it, in the politics of the family. For instance, among many of the peoples of Southern Africa it is believed to be taboo for women to work with cattle and hence they do not. Such taboos and prohibitions do not generally operate further north in East Africa, for instance amongst pastoral peoples there. Among Christian families in all societies, monogamy is the norm and polygamy is considered contrary to the teachings of the Church. In some societies it is forbidden by the secular law. More particular differences in familial politics may be explained within one society (or classes in it) in terms of the specific ideology and outlook of father and mother. For instance, do they have strong views about advancement and success? Do they want their children to be 'upwardly mobile'? Or are they less concerned about such matters and happy to see their children follow in their footsteps? Such considerations will strongly affect the internal politics of a particular family, perhaps influencing the way resources are used, for instance the amount put away in savings to enable a son (more commonly than a daughter? and if so, why?) to go on to higher education – and so forth.

I have gone on at some length with this example in order to show how one might deploy the analytical framework to achieve a fairly clear picture of the politics of a particular family or of the more general patterns of family politics in particular societies, or certain sections of them – whether these be castes, classes, ethnic groups or urban and rural communities and so forth. We have barely begun to understand the politics of the family. And although very important work has been done on some of these questions by anthropologists and sociologists – and more recently in a more committed and sometimes interdisciplinary fashion by feminists – it has seldom been the case that such activities of co-operation and conflict over resource use and distribution in families have been thought of *as* politics, and certainly not studied as such by the discipline of Politics. The scope for advance and research here is enormous.

Using the analytical framework, one might take one's interest in such local matters further and look at the politics of *groups* of families. The focus of analysis might be a nomadic hunter-gatherer band, and one could analyse the activities of co-operation and conflict over the use and distribution of resources amongst them, such as hunting and gathering activities and the politics of distribution of the product of such work.[7] Or it might be a more sedentary agricultural village. For example one

---

[7]   On hunter-gatherer or 'band' societies see, for instance, Eleanor Leacock and Richard Lee (eds), *Politics and History in Band Societies* (Cambridge, 1982).

might focus on the politics of differential access of distinct castes within an Indian village to resources such as land and water, and the politics associated with the introduction of a new well in one. [8] Or it might be a public or private housing estate in Britain. What are the common and what are the private resources here? What issues of conflict emerge on it? How are they resolved? In each instance the interplay of resource use and distribution with the other factors of power, social organization, culture and ideology will both influence and reflect the outcome. *That's* politics.

What of politics in institutions? The same analytical framework will help to disclose the character of their politics. Anyone who works in an institution – whether a factory, school, bureaucracy or office – will immediately recognize that its co-operative activities and disputes are fundamentally and regularly concerned with how resources should be used, and by whom and for what purposes. That's politics. The issues may have to do with facilities for the employees, or time off, or the allocation of offices and desks and so on. The ebb and flow of these activities, and the outcome of the disputes, are everywhere and always the outcome of the relations between the five elements discussed above: resource use and control; the structure of power and the systems of social organization, culture and ideology.

More widely, in a community, there may be local or national arguments about the use and distribution of public and private resources – as between playgrounds, crèches or car-parks; or between housing and defence; or wages and investment. These are not just random eruptions of conflict. They flow directly from the five elements, and their outcome will in turn be determined by the interplay of these in any given instance. That's politics. The same is true for discussions in tennis clubs or bowls clubs, for example, whether savings (or loans) should be spent on building more courts or greens, or building a new club-house. And that's politics.

Moreover, it is important to recognize that what is *really* going on in the course of 'industrial disputes', so called, is politics too. For these are conflicts about what different classes or groups (workers and managers/owners, for instance, or even different sections of workers) believe to be the proper or fair use and distribution of resources within the enterprise. These disputes may have to do with the introduction of

[8] An account of this for Bangladesh may be found in the useful short book by Betsy Hartmann and James Boyce, *Needless Hunger* (San Francisco, 1979).

new machines (possibly threatening some jobs), investment, facilities, holidays or wages. In analysing the politics of such disputes one needs to identify the different groups and their positions in relation to the control or ownership of the major productive resources; their access to, or capacity to use, power (of different kinds) in the course of decision-making about these matters; their relations to each other in terms of the structure of social organization; and the respective cultures and ideologies which help them to cohere and which both guide and reflect their particular interests and proposals.

Finally, in looking at the politics of whole societies at a much more aggregate and general level of analysis, the same approach is valuable. For if one wants to understand the *politics* of a society (not simply its *government*) it is not enough to follow the conventional approaches and to focus on the institutional arrangements and formalized public political struggles around them. For although an understanding of these is of course *part* of what is necessary, it is essential to look at the wider substantive and central issues of co-operation and conflict over the national use and distribution of resources; the national structures of power governing this (and *not only* in the public sector); the associated systems of social organization, culture and ideology. And in order to comprehend these, and the relations between them in the politics of the society, it is necessary to analyse matters which are not confined to the officially public and institutional realm. Thus, for instance, many Latin American societies are 'unstable' in their politics, *not* because civil governments and military regimes seem to circulate regularly within them with much speed. That is merely a symptom. But (on the application of the analytical framework) because even the most casual glance at the evidence will show that there is massive inequality in the control, ownership and distribution of resources; the structure of social organization is often sharply hierarchical in terms of classes (and sometimes ethnicity goes along with this); and that, accordingly, radically contrasting cultures and conflicting ideologies have coagulated around these. That so much force (usually applied by the military) is required to suppress and contain the discontent which seethes around these distributive inequalities seems hardly surprising. Similar patterns may be discerned increasingly in post-colonial Africa and many parts of Asia. Without looking at the kinds of factors proposed by this analytical framework, these patterns are simply unintelligible.

What is required in the analysis of the politics of such third-world societies is required also for understanding the historical and contemporary politics of the societies of the first and second worlds, and the relations between them. By asking each of the main questions outlined earlier – and preferably tracing their relations historically – one may gain a clearer picture of their contemporary politics, their antecedents and the sources of their current problems. Then, by assessing the similarities and contrasts between these analyses, one may begin to move towards a more systematic and richer approach to comparative political analysis of both historical and contemporary societies, and the relations between them.

6

It is a further and final part of my purpose here to suggest that the conception of politics elaborated here can not only be used in the analysis of all groups, institutions and societies, but also of problems which occur in them, and which are seldom considered by students in Politics departments. Such problems include unemployment, crime and certain forms and patterns of disease; as well as poverty, famines and ecological catastrophes.[9] The point can only be touched on here, but is worth making because these are all problems which need to be explained politically. For at the root of all such problems are the ways in which resources are used, produced and distributed. Some examples will help to make the point.

Unemployment, for instance, is not a mysterious blight which afflicts societies without cause or warning. Yet it is often treated in the media as if it were somehow a technical failure in the engine of the 'economic system' or the fault of some equally unexplained phenomenon or distant agent – like 'the world recession', or the Japanese or Germans or the like. Its analysis is generally confined to specialists in Economics, and is seldom thought of politically.[10] Yet it is obviously the case that it is a direct result of the way in which resources (private capital, public funds,

---

[9]   Some further illustrations of ecological and allegedly 'natural' disasters may be found in Leftwich, *Redefining Politics*, ch. 6; and also see Donald Worster, *Dust Bowl: The Southern Plains in the 1930s* (New York and London, 1979).

[10]   There has, of course, been work done on the politics of unemployment which is important, but systematic interdisciplinary work is uncommon, and it is still not a prime concern of students of Politics. See, for instance, Bernard Crick (ed.), *Unemployment* (London, 1981); and Brian Showler and Adrian Sinfield (eds), *The Workless State* (Oxford, 1981).

machines and raw materials) are owned, controlled, used and distributed – locally, regionally, nationally and globally. This is in turn directly bound up with certain kinds of productive cultures ('economic cultures', if one wishes) and ideologies, which institutionalize and stress, for instance, the power of private or state ownership or control of vast resources. Such power is exercised in pursuit of private or corporate profitability in the competitive politics of the world. Moreover, the *distribution* of unemployment in any society (systematically more concentrated amongst the poorer and weaker sections of the community) is in turn directly related to the structure of power and systems of social organization, and in turn affects these. To make the point starkly, unemployment has simply not been found amongst societies of hunter-gatherers, mixed cultivators or pastoralists, or indeed in any society – past or present – where there is more or less equal communal access to the resources which can sustain life. In short, it has only been with the emergence of increasingly private control of what were formally communal resources and opportunities, plus the rise of the state, that unemployment has emerged in human history, culminating in the dramatic forms it has come to take in the twentieth century especially.

The same general argument applies to the great epidemics of the nineteenth century in England, for instance – those of scarlet fever, measles, diphtheria, tuberculosis, smallpox and cholera. They were directly associated with the social, residential and sanitary conditions of the slums which, in turn, were directly linked with the new organization of production in the factory system, and the uneven distribution of resources amongst the people. Today, the social conditions which have brought about the modern epidemics – heart disease, cancers, bronchitis and accidents – can in turn be directly traced to our politics, that is to our systems of production and distribution, and to the cultures they promote in terms of lifestyles and consumption patterns. Moreover, the *distribution* of the causes of death in Britain is remarkably uneven and differs clearly from class to class, running along the contours of social organization as generated by the productive system and its associated divisions of labour and structures of power. For all these reasons, it is important to recognize that politics plays a major role in determining the kinds and distribution of diseases in societies. Likewise it can, and must, be the crucial factor in preventing it: 'medicine' alone will not. [11]

The same is true for famine. Now it is of course the case that droughts and floods which often precipitate famines are usually the direct result of natural factors. But the famines which may follow are not. They are much more clearly the result of the uneven distribution of resources in societies – a central outcome of their politics – which make certain groups (usually the poor and the powerless) *much more* vulnerable to the vicissitudes of nature than others – as the floods in Bangladesh and the drought in Ethiopia in the early 1970s illustrated so clearly. To ask the question 'Why is it that the poor and the weak are always the victims of famine?' – often when there is *as much food* available in the society as a whole as in previous non-famine years – is to ask not a technical question but a *political* one. [12]

Thus in seeking to explain the causes and character of these and other problems, it is necessary to recognize that they are not simply 'technical' or 'natural' problems. They are problems whose causes, conditions and consequences involve the interplay of natural, human and other resources, and whose relations are organized by the agency of human beings in their *politics*. They can only be resolved politically, though this will of course include technical solutions, but only as part of political ones. The analysis of such problems is not only a legitimate one but a necessary one for students of Politics. Again, at least as a starting point, the framework of analysis suggested here can provide powerful insights into the politics of such problems, and some indications of their prevention or solution.

7

In conclusion I hope that this brief account will help readers to think about politics as an activity which is far wider, much richer and certainly more interesting and important than its usual identification with

[11]   On health issues in Britain, the most important recent publication to emerge is the 'Black Report' or the *Report of the Working Group on Inequalities in Health,* chaired by Sir Douglas Black for the Department of Health and Social Security (London, 1980). This has now been edited and abridged in Peter Townsend and Nick Davidson (eds), *Inequalities in Health* (Harmondsworth, 1982). For more global and third-world health issues see Mike Muller, *The Health of Nations* (London, 1982); and Lesley Doyal (with Imogen Pennell), *The Political Economy of Health* (London, 1979).

[12]   See, for example, Amartya Sen, *Poverty and Famines* (Oxford, 1982).

governments and public affairs. My hope, too, is that the framework suggested in this chapter will enable people to study more systematically the politics of everyday life, in all groups and institutions they may be familiar with or interested in, whether it be in their families, clubs, departments, colleges, offices and factories; or in national terms, past or present, at home or abroad. In so doing, it will soon become clear how limiting and confining are the conventional boundaries and substantive concerns of the discipline of Politics, and how necessary it is to open up the disciplinary frontiers to a much fuller and freer interdisciplinary movement of evidence and explanation. It is not easy, to be sure. The whole terrain is a *political* and intellectual minefield, dotted with institutional jealousies and border police, with well-placed and often concealed booby-traps, diversions and dead-ends. Some people who attempt to work in such areas never seem to emerge alive. Those who do, often re-emerge tattered and in such a state of shock that they never seem able to say anything about any concrete politics or problems of the world again. But it has been done and can be done.[13] No one ever claimed that social science is easy, or that the politics of human societies are simple. They are not. Nonetheless, the more people that try, the better. For they will help to expand the study and understanding of politics in human societies in a way that may help to prevent the discipline of Politics from withering, stagnating or becoming irrelevant. In so doing they may also help to make us all more self-conscious of our politics so that we shall become more able, as communities, to *participate* actively in their management and improvement, wherever we may live or work. And that's highly political.

[13]   See some of the references cited under Further Reading for this chapter.

5

The levels of politics

ANDREW DUNSIRE

1

This chapter will explore a paradox, and then follow the chain of reasoning where it leads. The paradox is this. 'Politics' is generally understood as the way great affairs of state are settled, the way a nation resolves its differences and arrives at its choices — in a country like Britain, by processes of debate and discussion among elected representatives, which we think of as 'democratic'. Being 'democratic' is desirable, and the high principles of liberty, fairness and rights are the stuff of political discourse. A Member of Parliament is a kind of celebrity in his constituency, invited to important functions, generally treated with formal marks of respect such as one would accord to high-ranking churchmen or military men. The Palace of Westminster (which is the proper name for the building where the House of Commons and the House of Lords meet) is a noble building, and MPs are given a privilege accorded to no one else save Royalty: traffic is stopped to allow them to enter and leave the Parliament precincts. It would appear that Members of Parliament are held in high esteem, are Very Important People: and that they perform tasks of prime significance in the life of the nation.

On the other hand, common experience informs us, as we listen to talk in buses and pubs, or in our own homes and schools, that quite contrary to all that, 'politicians' are very often held in *low* esteem, that they are not taken seriously; and that politics is a 'dirty game', or all a matter of 'personalities', or of constant bickering and abuse of the other side. To 'play politics' with a question is to avoid tackling it squarely. 'Politicking' is a somewhat contemptible practice concerned with manoeuvring, buttonholing, log-rolling, suborning, bribing, and various other unscrupulous methods of winning a vote. Politics is petty, trivial, ephemeral and ridiculous. Politicians have a bad name in almost every western democratic country.

Now the point about paradoxes is that both the conflicting propositions are *true*. It is simple to produce an *apparent* paradox by contrasting a description of an ideal state of affairs with a description of the real state of affairs; 'politics *should* be noble, but they *are* petty' is not a paradox at all. We have to begin from the understanding that 'politics' is at once important and trivial, and that 'politicians' are both worthy of respect and worthy of scorn. That is a real paradox. But paradoxes have explanations. Most paradoxes result from putting side by side descriptions drawn from different frames of reference, looking at different aspects of the matter. In the present instance, the key to the resolution of the paradox, it will be suggested, is to be found in distinguishing between two levels of appreciation of the activity of politics and of politicians. And that resolution prompts the further question: how many other 'levels of appreciation' of political activity are there?

Before coming to that, however, it is worth noting that 'politics' has had its bad name, its pejorative connotation, since the sixteenth century at least. The *Oxford English Dictionary* has 'scheming, crafty, cunning; diplomatic, artfully contriving or contrived', for 1580. Machiavelli is the archetypal 'adviser of princes', or statesmen. There is an art in *timing* a suggestion. Deliver good news yourself; let others bear bad news. Do not simply advance the claims of your client; rather find some public interest whose pursuit will achieve the same end. And so on. There are undoubtedly 'arts of politics'.

A related idea that also has its respectable and disreputable sides is that of *rhetoric*. Aristotle defined it as 'the faculty of discovering the possible means of persuasion in reference to any subject whatever'.[1] Now it tends to be used to mean speech that does not persuade at all, because it is so familiar and predictable; routine oratorical flourish or weary sloganizing. Whereas politicians should discuss policies and matters of principle, and so educate the people (it may be thought), instead they 'indulge in empty rhetoric', or worse, 'mere slanging matches'. As

---

[1] Aristotle, *Art of Rhetoric*, Book 1, Section 2.1.

Bernard Crick put it in an article during the 1983 British general election campaign:

> Pericles remarked: 'The secret of liberty is courage', and in this general election campaign we will need all the courage we can screw up in face of a largely disgusting and discrediting way of conducting political debate . . . . The only mode of political discourse is charge and counter-charge, accusation and rebuttal, and a continuing pseudo-statistical rhetoric of rival figures on arbitrary time-scales about employment, investment, public expenditure, school attendance, indictable offences, prices since joining Europe, hospital building and closure. I just take topics from yesterday's BBC *Today* morning show . . . . Ordinary people realise that many things are very complicated, but they do not welcome being talked down to on this massive scale: very little attempt is made to simplify issues intelligently, politicians simply attack each other . . . . Politics is too serious a business for politicians alone . . . .[2]

Anthony Trollope was saying something very similar a hundred years ago, through his 'Palliser' novels: 'What does it matter who sits in Parliament? The fight goes on just the same. The same half-truths are spoken. The same wrong reasons are given. The same personal motives are at work.'[3]

'Politics is all "personalities" now' is perhaps the commonest charge. A reviewer of Richard Crossman's *Backbench Diaries* warned against politicians who lecture us on the overriding importance of issues and principles in politics:

> For the theme that emerges most strongly from these diaries, as dominant as the blues in a Cezanne landscape, is the overwhelming importance of personalities in politics. Naturally, politicians like to pretend that the opposite is true, which is why a Supergrass like Crossman is so valuable to us, the governed . . . . Naturally, they are inclined to blame the press for trivialising their debates, for concentrating on character rather than policy. This fascinating book is the proof that the press is right, and that it will be largely through the study of their personalities, emotions and whim that we regain control of our masters.[4]

---

[2] Bernard Crick, 'Meditation in Time of Sorrow', *The Times Higher Education Supplement*, 20 May 1983.

[3] Anthony Trollope, *Phineas Redux* (1874), quoted in Roy Hattersley, 'Endpiece: The Feast of St. Anthony', *Guardian*, 11 December 1982.

[4] Simon Hoggart, reviewing *The Backbench Diaries of Richard Crossman*, edited by Janet Morgan (London, 1981), in *Guardian*, 2 March 1981.

These comments do not, of course, dispose of the role of the media in the treatment of politics, which is a study in itself; nor do they explain the paradox we are considering. Is it *really* the case that no politicians now take a stand on issues of principle, that ideology is dead, that emotions and whim are in some way distinct from and unconnected with policy? Are there no differences that matter between left and right, or between either of those and the centre? Of course there are: and politicians embody them.

The differences of opinion that divide the Labour Party in Britain, which might look like 'intraparty squabbling' if you do not take the trouble to try to understand them, are based on profound analyses of society and of human nature, which produce different recommendations about how to proceed towards the goal of a fundamentally changed society, which both sides share. Within the Conservative Party in Britain, there are quite similar cleavages also based upon views of human nature and society, and there is perhaps less agreement on what sort of society would be a good one. Within the Social Democratic Party and Liberal Party Alliance, it may well be differences about the analysis of human nature and society, rather than about programme and manifesto, which make some Liberals oppose other Liberals, and some Social Democratic Party (SDP) members oppose other members, on the question of whether the Alliance should become a single party. Though it is not the place here to investigate these matters further, we can take it, I am sure, that none of the views or positions is trivial, or matters of personality, emotions and whim.

Why, then, is the opinion that they *are* such a persuasive one? It can only be because there is plenty of evidence in its favour; things we all see and hear that seem to fit that kind of explanation when it is proffered. Let us look at that evidence.

2

Let us accept as a working definition that 'politics' is what politicians do. Observed entirely from the outside, by non-politicians, 'politics' becomes a form of entertainment or diversion, the doings of politicians reported in the same spirit as the doings of pop stars and tennis stars: if they are 'famous', they are fair game. And it is undeniable that what goes on in the House of Commons, at party and trade union conferences, at weekend rallies and meetings of the party faithful, is 'politics'. What goes on in the legendary 'smoke-filled rooms' (we may have to find a new metaphor) and lobbies associated with such gatherings must also be accepted as 'politics', even if that is not so easily observable; diligent journalists and commentators excel in piecing together accounts of such behind-the-scenes discussions, the bargaining, the dealing in block votes, the horse-trading which precedes elections to the leadership and the executive, and so on. The more up-market Sunday newspapers go in for highly intelligent 'political analysis' of the week in Westminster and elsewhere, following the fortunes of this or that Minister as a speech flops or a reply to a debate wins acclaim, or the eclipse of the anti-Thatcherite 'Wets' in the Conservative party, or the outlines of the next Cabinet reshuffle, or the 'leadership struggle' in the Labour Party – there is always a current theme which is also a recurrent theme. It is by no means mere gossip; there is often serious and penetrating analysis of shifts of allegiance, and profound assessment of the role of an individual politician of some influence – Lord Whitelaw (epitome of the squirearchy), perhaps, or Enoch Powell, the eternal maverick.

What the ubiquity of the mass media treatment of 'politics' in this way masks is that this is a *spectator* sport. What is being observed, reported, discussed and evaluated is what politicians are doing amongst themselves. In spatial terms, it is a remarkably small world. We may think of it as 'at national level', but in fact it all takes place within a square mile or two in the capital city, in the area (if we are talking about London) between Euston Road in the north and Walworth Road across the river; except when British politics goes to the seaside in the late summer, for the party conferences in Brighton or Blackpool. If you do not move easily and confidently as an insider in these places, then you get your 'national politics' at second hand. And you can be forgiven for wondering what it all has to do with you.

What is going on, and is being reported in these ways in the press and television coverage, has to be understood in the light of two propositions about politics as an activity of politicians. One is that politics is about power.[5] The other is that politics is but one way of determining what the collectivity should do next about something.

Power-seeking, for oneself, or for what the possession of power by one can do for those one wishes to help, or for what one believes in, may

[5] See Further Reading for references.

or may not be disreputable. You may feel that decent people do not seek power, though they may be willing to have it thrust upon them. The fact remains that governments *must* wield power; if some persons do not occupy the seats of governmental power, others will; and the best the rest of us can do may be to ensure that those who do occupy these seats have achieved their positions by the accepted means, and have to render an account for their use of them. Whatever your motivation for being 'in politics', you will need power of some sort to realize these aims. But in the first place it is not power in the country that you need or seek: it is power in the party, a powerful position among politicians. That is what all the jockeying and the manoeuvring is about; and *it is inescapable.* The only major difference between now and earlier centuries, right up to the time of Gladstone and Chamberlain in Victorian England, is that we (the spectators) are now treated to a grandstand view of it all, with close-ups and action replays and learned analytical commentary – as if what we are seeing is all there is to be seen. The great statesmen of the past did not have such exposure. They spoke less often, they could afford more aloofness, and government was more of an arcane mystery. It is constant mass coverage that 'undoes' modern politicians. Better and more widespread general education, TV in every living-room, as well as the 'human interest' penchant of popular journalism, combine to make sure every politician has feet of clay. *Serious* political debate about principle is not entertaining enough, unless done by star performers.

The second proposition is that politics (here meaning decision as a result of debate and discussion and voting) is only one way of arriving at collective decisions. March and Simon, in a book that is not primarily about politics, make an illuminating suggestion.[6] This is that if a group of people find themselves in a difficulty about what they should collectively do concerning a particular problem, they progressively try four ways out (before resorting to a fifth): (1) problem-solving; (2) persuasion; (3) bargaining; and (4) 'politics' or perhaps 'politicking'. (The fifth way is violence.)

In *problem-solving*, all of the group have the same objectives; and, if they pool their information and their ingenuity, the chances are that they will find a solution to their difficulty which is satisfactory to all of them, like solving a puzzle together.

[6]   James G. March and Herbert A. Simon, *Organizations* (New York, 1958), p. 130.

If they do not all have the same objectives, problem-solving will not work, for what might be an acceptable solution for some will not be for others. But if *some* objectives are shared, one may try inducing the others to relax some of their requirements for the sake of achieving the rest. This is the *persuasion* mode.

Bargaining occurs when objectives are not shared and no one can be persuaded to surrender goals unilaterally, but will tradeoff (so much of your objectives for so much of mine), enabling a solution fully satisfactory to no one but where no one goes away empty-handed.

If even bargaining does not produce a solution, what March and Simon call 'politics' may emerge. I see this as having three components: (1) altering the definition of the group; (2) altering the definition of the problem; (3) altering the definition of the solution – sometimes all three together.

You alter the definition of the group if you can bring in some more people, or remove the problem to a superior body or larger arena – in the way that wage negotiators go back 'for instructions' to their principals, or in the way the House of Commons 'goes to the people'.

You alter the definition of the problem if you relate it in some way to a more general problem (make it only a special case of a wider issue), so as to try to shift the ground of argument, or change people's thinking about it (and possibly their allegiance); as when support is mobilized for selling off public housing for rent by reference to a 'property-owning democracy'. (This is what the phrase 'making a political issue out of it' refers to: you align the present difficulty with the standard party alignment on problems and their solutions, so far as you can.) You may then recruit as allies people who know nothing at all about the original difficulty but will side with you for solidarity's sake.

Finally, you alter the definition of the solution if you accept one that is satisfactory not to all, even if at a low level of aspiration, but satisfactory to a *majority*. This is quite a big step and we should pause over it.

Comparing majority decision to problem-solving (often called 'rational decision-making'), or even to bargaining (as found in 'the market'), it is clear enough that 'counting heads', as a way of bringing a conflict over objectives to an end, is not a function of reason or even of discussion, but simply an alternative to '*breaking* heads'. It is, of course, an infinitely preferable alternative. The key to its understanding is the implied agreement of the minority (or minorities) to accept the solution which gains a majority – at least for the time being; they have not been convinced, or persuaded, or bought off. Indeed, the appeal to *authority* of any kind, as a way of bolstering an argument or resolving an impasse, falls into the same category. It too, therefore, is a specifically *political* kind of solution.

With these understandings, we may see both how the way of 'politics' is in some senses less desirable than other ways of arriving at collective decisions, and how (to invert Clausewitz) politics is nothing but the resolution of conflict by other means than war – and much more desirably.[7] Though a long way from a 'rational' solution, the way of politics is certainly better than the terrorist or military way.

'Majority rule' *is* democracy for most people. Yet it is noticeable that in collective decision-making arenas in 'private' life, in clubs and churches and perhaps university governing bodies and the like, the feeling is often quite overtly articulated that a majority decision is second best. Solutions ostensibly satisfactory to all are preferred; rational problem-solving is the only fully respectable mode. So what happens is that the persuading, bargaining and coalition-building has to be done *outside* the formal arena, beforehand; kites are flown over coffee, influential individuals are squared, words are judiciously dropped in the right ears, loyalty is appealed to, etc. – in order to preserve the fiction of rationality in the formal meeting.

This is politics, too: politics among politicians, even if not professional ones (recall the subtitle of Cornford's *Microcosmographia Academica:* 'a guide for the young academic politician'[8]); but with no television cameras to observe – and untrammelled by the paradox we began from, because nobody supposes that this kind of politics *has* any higher manifestations.

What we have been looking at in this section, then, is undeniably politics, for it is what politicians are seen doing, *qua* politicians; but it is *politics among politicians* – insider politics. The rest of us are only looking on. And we have to be sure we can interpret correctly what we are seeing. Take one illustration: Question Time in the House of Commons. Anyone who thinks this is a time when MPs hold Ministers to account for the behaviour of their colleagues and civil servants does not have a chance of understanding what actually happens in the House.

[7] Karl von Clausewitz, 'Der Krieg ist nichts als eine Fortsetzung der Politischen Verkehr mit Einmischung anderer Mittel' (*Vom Krieg*, p. 888), in *Oxford Dictionary of Quotations* (Oxford, 3rd edn, 1979), p. 152.

[8] F. M. Cornford, *Microcosmographia Academica, Being a Guide for the Young Academic Politician* (Cambridge, 1908).

This is a game MPs play with one another; and it is a *participant* sport this time, not a spectator sport. Only the players are in a position to see the game properly, and to appreciate the finer points of the play. What the rest of us think of it is irrelevant. Hence, also, the appalling failure of Parliamentary broadcasting in Britain. MPs basically do not *care* what they sound like; they are performing *to each other*. The same is true of the rostrum speeches at party and trade union conferences. These are intrinsically private occasions, the speeches are not for our hearing; we are eavesdropping. Insider politics again, with little indeed to do with 'the representation of the people', or the 'grand inquest of the nation', or the 'great debate' on questions of the day. Indeed, this kind of politics is *almost* not about policy at all.

We have noted that there is a surprisingly restricted spatial dimension to this kind of politics. If we examine the *time* dimension, this is the level at which, in Harold Wilson's words, 'a week is a long time in politics.' The scene shifts daily, the passage of time is marked by press and broadcasting deadlines, the pace of change is rapid. Insider politics are volatile.

3

But politicians are not always talking amongst themselves. They also talk to us, the non-politicians – and that too, by our working definition, is 'politics'. Especially at election times, but continuously at a somewhat lower intensity, politicians of all parties lose few opportunities of 'putting their case to the people', of persuading us to continue to support the party in government or not to do so. This is by and large a different kind of politics. A different language is used, when you are trying to structure the perceptions and influence the loyalties of non-politicians, than when you are talking to your fellow party members or to other politicians. It is a more *public* language. (It is true that politicians often use this 'public' language when speaking in the House of Commons or at party conferences, but this is because what they are saying is 'for public consumption' and not really directed at their immediate audience – a fact which is well appreciated by them.) This 'public' level of politics is the level of 'party politics', of policies and programmes, of manifestos and platforms, of beliefs and creeds.

It is also the level on which we – the non-politicians – struggle to formulate our own political outlook (if we do). We debate (in British politics) whether what recent Labour governments did was true socialism, and what the difference between social democracy and democratic socialism might be. We consider whether being a Conservative entails being a monetarist or the opposite, and what link there is between a stand against further immigration and the 'privatization' of public property.

This, to paraphrase the former British Prime Minister Edward Heath, is the acceptable face of politics, the more or less honest clash of principle. Of course, it is difficult to disentangle principle from *interest*: certainly, being of a party (or voting for one) because you believe in its doctrines is not incompatible with voting for it because it will be to your personal benefit to have that party in power; though there *are* perhaps people who will (in this sense) vote for principle and *against* their interests. It is probably fair to say that many voters and party members would be genuinely unable to distinguish the interests that (in the perception of others) permeate their sincerely held views. Kenneth Hudson suggests that:

> to the Presidents of many Women's Institutes in rural areas of Britain, Conservative politics were not politics at all. To hold Conservative views was as natural as breathing and eating, so natural and God-given, indeed, that the rule about no politics or religion at Institute meetings was assumed to apply only to the introduction of socialist ideas into the peaceful Wednesday evening atmosphere.[9]

In the twenties and thirties, similarly, there was much bluster about the 'introduction of politics into local government', and the cry can even now be heard in other areas of social life.

For present purposes, it is not necessary to distinguish between 'the clash of principle' and the 'interplay of interests' (or the 'grinding of axes') as the stuff of politics on this level, for either they are aspects of one another, or they are alternative orthodoxies of democratic politics ('adversarial politics' or 'pluralist politics'); and whichever way one looks at it, the politics one is observing or participating in is politics on this second or 'public' level, as contrasted with 'insider politics'.

'Public' politics are not as spatially concentrated as insider politics.

---

[9]   Kenneth Hudson. *The Language of Modern Politics* (London, 1978), p. 1.

We think nationally; the area we have in mind is the area over which the government we acknowledge has jurisdiction. Political creeds or beliefs, for all their universalistic language, are surprisingly nation-specific in operational terms. You can test this by asking yourself whether, as a British Liberal or Conservative or Labour supporter, you could confidently deduce what a Dutch or Italian Liberal, etc., believes and recommends. There *are* continuities across frontiers, but one has to do one's homework on them, as British Members of the European Parliament found. Interests too are territorially rooted, for purely pragmatic reasons, though possibly the area of reference is more the national economy than the national polity; and there now are some Europe-wide pressure groups, responding to EEC policies.

There are, certainly, credal systems, such as Marxism or philosophical conservatism, which purport to transcend political frontiers and purely national social class systems. I will not dispute this here; insofar as such beliefs have the character of philosophies of history or religions, we will come to that later; insofar as Marxism or philosophical conservatism enters the political fray, as distinct from academic discussion, I would say that they do so in national costume.

The time-scale of change in 'public' politics is not so frenetic as in insider politics. People do not change their beliefs, or their interests, or the arguments for one policy rather than another, every week. Change is measured in months and years, marked broadly by the parliamentary timetable.

4

Now we are in a position to pursue this idea of different 'levels of appreciation' of politics where it might lead. If we can distinguish between 'insider politics' and 'public politics', are there things that politicians do which are on a different level again? And surely there are.

For instance: the Liberal/SDP Alliance in Britain has made it plain that if they should come to a position of power, one of the things they would do would be to alter the electoral system, and introduce proportional representation. Now this is in one sense part of their creed; but at the same time, altering the electoral system is not on all fours, as government policy, with selling public housing or regulating immigration. You could say it does not only alter the law, it alters the *constitution* (even though, in the United Kingdom, it is a change that could be made by the same procedures as a change in the ordinary law). It would certainly affect (it is specifically designed to affect) one of the basic characteristics of the British style of politics, what we call the 'two-party system', or 'adversarial politics'. The argument is that this format no longer matches the real pattern of British political forces, that it is time the 'mould' was broken.

Sometimes when you go abroad to a foreign country, you for the first time appreciate the oddness of some practice in your own country, which up until then you simply took for granted; just as we seldom are really conscious of certain vital processes in our own bodies, like breathing, until something goes wrong. Yet breathing is a *condition* of achieving any of our earthly purposes whatsoever, of all our conscious acts and choices. Similarly, the institutional settings of British politics, the rules and conventions of parliamentary government or the relative incorruptibility of our judges and civil servants, are the *conditions* of following one policy or another, serving one interest or another. We may take them for granted until they are brought to our attention: but they are all the time actually 'moulding' the ways we think about politics and the objectives we set for ourselves and our politicians. And if they are doing that, they are influencing our political thinking; so, they *are* 'politics' too.

This third level of politics is usually called the 'institutional' level, on which we (and here, particularly, 'we' means students and teachers of Politics) discuss differences in 'regime' or political system (presidential government, constitutional monarchy, the dictatorship of the proletariat) in terms of the organs and procedures which provide the setting for 'politics' on the second level and the first level. I want to make two points.

The first is that when we are dealing with human social systems, the familiar language of distinguishing between the 'structure' and the 'behaviour' within that structure may mask more than it reveals. If 'structure' is thought of as like the skeleton (bone structure) of a person, or like the load-bearing walls and beams of a building, then an organization or complex of organizations *has* no 'structure'; what it has is a 'framework' of rules, understandings, conventions or expectations, some of which are more 'basic', well established or permanent than others. Some expectations are so firm as to be taken for granted. These are 'institutions'.

What we take for granted we tend to suppose permanent or un-changing, even inescapable. Institutions change more slowly than the more ephemeral manifestations of political activity, indeed; but they are 'activities' themselves nevertheless, in *continuous creation* and adaptation, as their human mediators respond (perhaps with considerable time-lag) to changes in the life around them.

The second point is that any particular institution or organization (seen as a persisting or handed-down configuration of rules and expectations) is also an expression of *values*: a 'mix' of a number of values in certain proportions – values such as (in the present context) the weight to be given to majority decision or to authority, to privilege or expertise, to knowledge or wealth, and so on.

Perhaps this can be more easily appreciated on the scale of the firm, or the university or the like, rather than the polity as a whole. The internal 'structure' of such an organization – the departmentalization, the hierarchy, the procedures – can be perceived as a statement of the modes of decision-making, degree of specialization, channels of communication and so on, which the designers either consider appropriate or take for granted as necessary. The outcome is a specific pattern of authority, power, rights and privileges that forms a kind of 'signature' or characteristic mark of the organization.

It is a fascinating field for comparative study, whether as between individual organizations of the same broad type (e.g. universities or schools), or as between organizations of different types (e.g. comparing manufacturing firms with hospitals), which is called Organization Theory. It is intuitively clear that the institutional fabric does condition beliefs about the approach to the resolution of conflict of objectives that will be successful in such places; we, as it were, know 'how to behave' in them to a remarkable extent even if we have never been there before. Indeed, there are often devices to guide our reactions built into the bricks-and-mortar (or steel and plastic) of some organizations: consider the layout of a supermarket, or of the House of Commons, or the imposing facade of a bank. These speak quite plainly (if subliminally) of the values of the designers.

This, then, is what I would wish to mean by the *institutional* level of politics; the conditioning or management of second-level political activity by the institutionalization of particular patterns of relevant values – who is to have authority to do what by what procedures.

Describing the spatial dimension of this level of politics is less simple than for the earlier two levels. On the one hand, the institutionalization of these values is closely associated with national institutions and, to a degree at least, different from polity to polity. On the other hand, the idea of 'political system' or 'type of regime' is inherently comparative, and similarities based on historical factors can be found crossing political frontiers – the 'Westminster communion', or the countries of the common law tradition, or the countries of the Napoleonic heritage, the various imperial legacies, and so on. Perhaps we can indicate this by thinking of 'cross-national spheres of influence'. The time-scale of change on this level is relatively slow: let us say, over decades.

5

If you are following the train of thought, you will now be ahead of me. The next question obviously is: where do these 'values' come from? What conditions these patternings? Is there a yet deeper level of 'politics'?

Yes. In any society, big or small, there are common appreciations spoken or unspoken that are so fundamental as to be even more deeply subconscious than the 'taken-for-grantedness' of institutions. They can be said to *constitute* the society, to make it what it is, give it its salient characteristics, mark it off from other societies. These appreciations include the society's ideas about property and possessions, attitudes to the family and to elders and children, sex roles, codes of right conduct in a large repertoire of social situations, dispositions towards strangers, notions of patriotism and attitudes towards aggression and warfare, measurements of 'success' and 'status', worship of gods; underpinning even these, ideas of how you establish truth, where wisdom resides, the causes of observed effects. All this is the subject-matter of Political Anthropology; and the term used for these complexes of learned perceptions and appreciations, with their beginnings in the cradle or its equivalent and reinforcement throughout life, is *culture*. There are different cultures, and it is extraordinarily difficult to communicate across cultural boundaries, or to be 'at home' in the politics of another culture than your own.

Let me stress that this 'socialization' process goes very deep, but there is very little that is truly *inherited* about it: that is, incorporated into the human genes. Skin colour and other bodily attributes of different peoples may, from experience, alert us to the possibility of difference of culture; but our attitudes to these bodily attributes (and characteristic behaviours) are part of our own cultural conditioning; they have been learned, and they have to be continually reinforced or 'taught', until they have been internalized and the taught can become the teachers. In this way the traditions are maintained and the essential integrity of the society preserved.

But not everything is continually renewed in this way; in every society, some customs and traditional attitudes are kept up, some are allowed to disappear. It is a selective process, though it would be foolish and mistaken to try to pinpoint who at any one time is doing the selecting. The conclusion, nevertheless, can only be that the various aspects of the cultural code which persist do so not because they come from the past, but because they are needed in the present.

The ceremonial surrounding so much of the proceedings of the House of Commons is kept up because it still has a point to make. Rituals, symbols, celebration of earlier events in the tribe's history, are also current political activity, 'appreciation management'. If the very stones of 'our cultural heritage' appear to speak to us across the centuries, it is a living human voice which is interpreting to us what they are saying. It was a quite commonplace and not necessarily unfriendly comment on the recent Royal Wedding of Prince Charles and Lady Diana Spencer to see it as a conscious, highly elaborate affirmation of certain priorities at this fourth level of politics in this country; and considered as rhetoric of a sort, it was surely highly successful. [10]

Rites and ceremonies, 'occasions' and rallies, commemorations and consecrations, whether overtly 'political' or not, are expressions of what is held dear at the fourth level: what does one revere, what does one shun, what does one emulate, what does one hold taboo. And again, this is not something fixed, unchanged since the dawn of time, but something dynamic and contemporary. This thought is neatly put in a book review of an illustrated history of the English 'gentleman':

> The history of an idea-system – and above all, a reigning one – cannot
> be so straightforwardly rendered as illustrative narrative. The reason is

[10] I am indebted to David Lloyd-Jones of the University of Glasgow for permitting me to read in draft a chapter of his forthcoming book on *Politics as Rhetoric*, in which he develops in particular the notion of a 'rhetoric of action' which may typify a political society as clearly as its habitual language usages. For example, the American Wild West frontier had its 'rhetoric of action' or of behaviour that marked it off from the more settled east.

that its meaning, its social authority, consists essentially in its
daily defeat of other and contending ideologies . . . . The
significance of dominant ideas and values is just *how* they
overcome their competitors . . . .[11]

As with institutions, there are at least two sets of boundaries in the
spatial dimension of cultures. On the one hand each historical
community or tribe-equivalent has its symbols and ceremonial rhetoric.
On the other hand, much larger communities share so many basic
attitudes on this level that communication is possible – certainly when
contrasted with the gulfs between them and other groupings. So we can
speak of the Judaeo – Christian ethic, or the Hellenic – Roman
tradition; but it is significant that often it is enough, in this kind of
discourse, to refer to the *continent*, and let it stand for these not-easily-
bridged gulfs. So 'Europeans', or 'the Africans', or in verb-form,
'Americanization'. The time-scale of change is possibly speeding up;
one would have said that it was measured century by century, except
that the use of that verb-form in the previous sentence reminds us that
nowadays, with the 'communications revolution' well established, it
can take only decades to alter even such basic matters as attitudes to the
family and to 'material goods'.

6

These four levels of 'politics' are summarized in table 5.1. The theory
of political activity set out in the preceding pages has two main theses:
the first is that each lower or deeper level of political activity constrains,
influences, infuses, enables and conditions political activity on the level
above. Our 'insider politics' in this country is, as it were, the outcome
of successive layers of structuring. So that although one can by no means
predict the specifics of day-to-day politics (being supremely subject to
the vagaries of the hour, the place and the persons), one can say that, at
least in the short term, our kind of politics could not be radically
different from what it is. The second thesis is this: that these layers of
structuring are not, as it were, the *deposits* of time, or of history and
geography; they are contemporary artefacts, which are continually
maintained. It is the *whole* that, in one sense, is current politics; political

[11] Tom Nairn, in a review (*Guardian*, 2 October 1981) of Mark Girouard, *The Return to Camelot:
Chivalry and the English Gentleman* (New Haven, 1981).

activity operates, consciously or not, on all levels at once. But the deeper layers are much *less* volatile than the superficial ones.

The explanation of the paradox with which we began is that the two views of politicians (that they are to be disparaged, that they are to be looked up to) belong on different levels. Non-politician observers are bombarded with images of politicians behaving and speaking in the ways that are 'natural' to them when amongst their own kind; they contrast these images with a second series of images of politicians behaving and speaking on the 'public' level, in the ways that are 'natural' when addressing and confronting non-politicians. The perceived gap between the two behaviours is misread (although confusedly) as a more familiar gap between normative utterances and actual conduct (like, perhaps, the preacher who 'falls from grace' in his personal life), and disillusion is the result. The 'dirty game' of power-seeking is compared with the 'noble ideals' to which public-level speakers appeal, and (again confusedly) the gap is seen as one between rhetoric and reality. The truth is that power-seeking, within the procedures and limits sanctioned by the institutional and cultural rules and expectations of the society, is 'functional' for the pursuit of noble ideals: if power in government would not be sought by game-playing of the kind disparaged, it would be attained by other means.

TABLE 5.1   THE LEVELS OF POLITICS

Level	Content	Space	Time
I Insider politics	in-House games; wheeler-dealing and bargaining; jobs and posts	capital; seaside conferences	day-to-day volatility
II Public politics	party programmes, beliefs, creeds; interest-articulation; elections, voting	national territory	months/ years
III Institutions	polity, regime; mix of dominant values – authority, participation, etc.	groupings of nations	decades
IV Culture	attitudes to e.g. family, property, national symbolic life; epistemology	continent	centuries
V Economy	production technology – hunter-gathering, agriculture, industrialization	hemisphere, planet	epochs

This is not to say that every tactic or ploy or manoeuvre in politics at the 'insider' level is as acceptable as another: some will contravene the law, others will go counter to the prevailing moral code, and insofar as conduct breaching these standards is what is referred to as 'the dirty game', or as 'politicking', then of course it is justifiably condemned. But this would not apply to *all* political manoeuvring, or to *all* power-seeking, or to *all* politicians, as the opening paradox had it. If only criminal politicians, or morally reprehensible political activity, are to be disparaged, then there is no paradox.

Similar 'perceived gaps' between quasi-ritual activity or symbolic persons on the one hand, and insider politics or even credal politics on the other, are also mistaken. A contrast between the conduct of the Royal Family and of representatives of the people, say, when the former are carrying out their public duties of a wholly ritual kind and the latter are engaged on essential interest-articulation work, cannot validly be expressed as a contrast between actions that are 'above politics' and 'political activity'. In the model presented here, the ritual actions *are* political activity, on a deeper level. Misperceptions of this kind can indeed lead to disillusion, disenchantment and dissatisfaction but only because there was illusion, enchantment and misplaced satisfaction in the first place.

It may well be, however, that not only changes in the *visibility* of insider politics, through greatly increased press and especially TV coverage, have contributed to these popular misperceptions, but also changes in the attitudes and attributes of politicians themselves. In many ex-colonial countries, it is asserted that there has been a deterioration in the quality of politicians and of political life, since the passing of the generation which fought for and achieved independence. The struggle for freedom ennobled politics generally, and 'insider politics', though never absent, had as their measure the one great goal. With its attainment, less worthy criteria obtain. Anthony King, in a recent article, shows that since 1945 in Britain there has been a distinct shift in the kind of people who serve in the House of Commons and in the Cabinet.[12] He distinguishes between 'career politicians' and others, meaning those so committed to the life as to have no other interests, as against those who are in politics but who could easily see themselves

---

[12]   Anthony King, 'The Rise of the Career Politician in Britain — and its Consequences', *British Journal of Political Science* 2(3) (1981), pp. 249 – 85.

doing something else. Since 1945, Cabinet and Commons have lost most of the second sort and have become almost completely dominated by the first sort, committed career politicians.

One danger is obvious: that politics becomes ever more cut off from what is usually in this context called 'real life', bereft of its leavening of people who bridge the gulf. Another is perhaps less obvious: that, as politics on the insider level consumes all energies (keeping the party nomination, keeping the whip, keeping the majority, keeping the parliamentary limelight), politics on the credal level comes to be seen as indeed secondary, a bit of an irrelevance, even a bit of a nuisance – all this going down to the constituency and talking endlessly about policies and principles. If the creed, the programme and even the interests, begin to take second place to the 'life', the game, then the non-politicians' perceptions of gap become valid. Politics that is too dominated by 'insider' concerns is soon seen as genuinely marginal to real life. People learn that the real and immediate influences on their lives are determined not in 'politics' but in something different called 'the economy', in which the politicians are seen as ineffectual, and in which they themselves are conscious only of powerlessness. Scepticism and cynicism about politics and most politicians is a quite rational response.

7

In addition to the four levels I have dealt with, modern political analysis uses a fifth and even deeper level of appreciation of political phenomena, which I shall label *economy* to avoid calling it 'production technology'. On this level, some scholars emphasize the significance of basic uses of natural resources, the patterns of which can be seen to underlie even culture and cultural differences. Thus all the political manifestations we have been discussing are seen as liable to alter, as the economic system changes from food-gathering to hunting, to primitive agriculture, to occupational division of labour and trading, to industrialization and urbanization, and now to what are called 'post-industrial' societies or possibly 'cybernetic' societies.

This is, of course, a theory of historical development. But it is also, and crucially, a categorization of contemporary societies across the present globe, and a purported theory of relationships between societies, based on the birth, growth, and struggle to survive of capitalism. It is highly controversial, and as explanatory theory there are problems about it.

But whether one takes that particular approach, or some other, one can hardly avoid the recognition of an arena of political activity that transcends all clashes even between cultures, let alone between regimes and creeds and individuals. There is now a class of problem to be dealt with only on the world scale: the problems of overpopulation and of food distribution, of energy and pollution, of endangered species (including, perhaps, *homo sapiens*) and non-renewable resources. These are planetary issues, and the planet is searching for ways to handle them – *sans* supporting rituals, *sans* effective institutions, *sans* motivating creeds, and interests; or rather, in the face of the existing rituals, institutions, creeds, and interests. There is an economics of planetary consumption and trade, but there seems no adequate politics, for use when the market fails.

In table 5.1, we insert for spatial dimension the planet Earth, or its hemispheres, east/west, north/south. The time-scale of change has been the era or historical epoch. But we do not know how many epochs we have to come.

The conclusion we *should* reach on the basis of this analysis is not an optimistic one. It is that political solutions to world problems are not likely, perhaps not possible, at least not in the foreseeable future, at least as politics are presently conducted. If the theory of how to understand politics in our own system is correct, then it is in principle correct also for every other political system, though of course we move up a different path through the levels in each case. The politicians who take the operative decisions in each country are constrained, imprisoned, by influences and demands derived in the same way. In every case, their response to any 'fifth level' stimulus will be conditioned by influences from their particular fourth, third and second levels of political activity.

Do we not see precisely this happening on every hand? Does not the evidence bear out the theory?

As we sit on the edge of nuclear annihilation due to the hemispherical lunacy we call the east versus west arms race, or contemplate the global 'agenda item' we call north versus south for fear of arousing the demons that attend its real name, the paradox we began from is seen as relatively trivial, of little importance. 'Who will speak for Earth?' Carl Sagan asked. Where is the ballot-box where we can cast a vote for sanity? Whom do we lobby, to make some difference? Where is the crucial arena, to mount demonstrations and hold marches? What can we *do*? If reason and persuasion do not work, and there is so little leverage to bargain with, is there really no *political* way either?

Let us hope that the analysis is wrong, and that although we cannot yet clearly recognize the signs, a new kind of politics is being born that will enable us to deal with these planetary problems. Students of Politics today have great responsibilities.

6

Political philosophy and politics

JOHN HORTON

1

Most departments of Politics in British universities offer courses in political philosophy, political theory or the history of political thought. In some departments at least one such course may be compulsory for undergraduates specializing in Politics. However, there is no very precise agreement about the meaning of these terms, and what is called political theory in one department might be called political philosophy in a second and the history of political thought in another, while within a single department these terms may be used to identify very different courses. While such varied terminology is no doubt disconcerting and confusing, particularly for the new student or non-specialist, it need not necessarily be of any greater import. However, with regard to this area of the study of politics, it is often symptomatic of a deeper uncertainty about the nature of the engagement itself. Furthermore, this picture is additionally complicated by the development of courses in methodology or the philosophy of the social sciences and courses concerned with the history or analysis of social theory, all of which have, at the very least, philosophical aspects.

Some distinctions in this area are therefore an essential preliminary to any account of the nature of political philosophy and its place in the study of politics, which is the subject of this essay. However, my approach to the issues raised will be for the most part loosely discursive rather than tightly argued, and such conclusions as there are should be treated as tentative and provisional. Only in the last part of the essay does the level of argument aspire to be more rigorous, though even there it is insufficiently detailed. However, there is perhaps less cause than might be thought for being apologetic about this, for it locates what follows in a long and worthy philosophical tradition in which the journey is more interesting than the destination and the questions more important than the answers.

2

Traditionally, the study of political theory, which I shall henceforth use as a generic term covering all the academic engagements within this area, has involved in some part the reading and examination of the 'great texts' such as Plato's *Republic*, Aristotle's *Politics*, Hobbes's *Leviathan*, Locke's *Second Treatise on Government*, Rousseau's *The Social Contract* and Hegel's *The Philosophy of Right*, to mention only some of the most important. These texts are among those usually thought of as the classics of political theory. However, precisely how they should be studied and the point of doing so are both often rather cloudy. Should they be studied from a primarily historical perspective, using the methods and practices of the historian to reconstruct the historical meaning of the texts? Or should they be approached philosophically as works purporting to offer general truths about the nature of political life and organization with a view to assessing the cogency of their reasoning, the uncovering of their assumptions and such like? Perhaps they should be regarded as incipient Political Science or Sociology now superseded by a much more methodologically sophisticated and self-conscious discipline of Political Science? Or perhaps a combination of some or all of these welded together to constitute a coherent enquiry? Certainly the texts themselves are usually an amalgam of what would now be thought of as philosophical analysis, sociological theorizing, historical explanation and practical recommendation, but this does not of course settle the question of what is possible for us.

I shall begin by very briefly trying to distinguish some of the activities that have been included within the broad area of political theory. However, my main purpose in doing so is to begin the process of identifying and characterizing a coherent and defensible conception of political philosophy, so what is said about other aspects of political theory will be sketchy in the extreme and subservient to this purpose. In particular, I shall distinguish four enquiries which will be called political philosophy, the history of political thought, social theory and the philosophy of the social sciences. The last is mentioned as one of the ways in which philosophy relates to the study of politics, but it is not a relationship which will be explored here at all. It is a topic that would require a separate essay to do it any sort of justice. In justification of this exclusion one may point out that the philosophy of the social sciences is generally thought of as being somewhat apart from the traditional concerns of political theory. However, this in no way diminishes its significance, rather the reverse, for insofar as it is concerned with the exploration of the different ways in which politics is studied, particularly the assumptions and procedures of political 'science', it has serious claims to lie at the heart of any undergraduate programme of political studies. However, my concern is with political philosophy and not the philosophy of the social sciences.

The purpose of these distinctions is to identify different kinds or forms of enquiry into politics. In the current fashion for inter-disciplinary study, these distinctions are often dismissed as arbitrary or positively obstructive of attempts to understand politics as a totality. However, one of the contentions of this essay is that an enquiry which is not a specific or particular kind of enquiry is a muddled enterprise, and that nothing is gained and a great deal is lost by confusing, for example, historical and philosophical enquiries. This is not to deny of course that there may be a hint of greyness at the borderlines or that it may not be valuable, or even essential, on occasion, to combine the results of different kinds of enquiry. My point is only that they are essentially different kinds of investigation with their own concerns, procedures, methods and criteria of adequacy. It is arguable, however, that the study of political theory often exhibits just such a muddle, and one line of criticism which has been advanced particularly powerfully over the last couple of decades stems from a school of historians who have wanted to insist upon the essentially historical character of the study of political theory.[1] On their view, the appropriate methods and procedures for studying political theory, and especially the 'great texts', are historical.

From this perspective the proper aim of the student of political theory should be the reconstruction of the historical meaning of political theories. What Plato, Locke or Hobbes meant in the *Republic*, *Second*

---

[1]   I have in mind especially Q. Skinner, J. Dunn and J. Pocock. Their works are too numerous to cite but a good place to start is Q. Skinner, 'Meaning and Understanding in the History of Ideas', *History and Theory* 8 (1969). A good example of the kind of work they were concerned to criticize is J. Plamenatz, *Man and Society*, 2 vols (London, 1963).

Treatise or *Leviathan* is a historical question which involves the recovery of the intentions which lay behind such texts. The texts therefore need to be understood in their historical setting of political events, and the debates and disputes with other contemporary theorists and ideologues. In short, the 'great texts' need to be understood as political acts themselves. They are contributions to an ongoing political debate and it is this context rather than that of the political or philosophical concerns of today that they need to be understood. In particular attention must be given to the language of political debate at the time to understand the range of possible expression open to a political theorist. This requires a detailed familiarity with both the major and lesser political writers of the period rather than a close reading of the texts themselves largely abstracted from that context. Thus much more relevant than a frequent rereading and puzzling over some apparently obscure passages in, for example, the *Leviathan*, is a familiarity with the works of contemporary pamphleteers, theorists and ideologues. Of course not all who advocate a primarily 'historical' approach to political theory would subscribe to a similar account of what constitutes proper historical method and there are serious objections to it which have not received wholly convincing replies. [2] However, whatever the precise details and refinements of the methodology, it cannot credibly be denied that there is a genuine historical enquiry identified here. What Plato, Hobbes or Locke meant in the *Republic, Leviathan* and *Second Treatise* is an interesting question which is, at least in principle, capable of being answered by historical enquiry, but it is neither the only nor obviously most important question that can be asked about them. We may be more interested in the cogency of the arguments and their continued relevance. Of course the cogency of arguments is not something which can be understood independently of their meaning, and there is here a meeting place for 'historical' and what I shall later identify as 'philosophical' concerns. However, the focus of interest might not be in whether this or that is precisely what, for example, Hobbes meant, but rather what is the most consistent interpretation of the arguments in the text; what are their presuppositions; whether they seem to offer

---

[2]   See, for example, C. D. Tarlton, 'Historicity, Meaning and Revisionism in the Study of Political Thought', *History and Theory* 12 (1973); R. Ashcraft, 'On the Problem of Methodology and the Nature of Political Theory', *Political Theory* 3 (1975); and B. Parekh and R. N. Berki, 'The History of Political Ideas: A Critique of Q. Skinner's Methodology', *Journal of the History of Ideas* 34 (1973).

a cogent understanding of political obligation or whatever. These questions are not historical and they indicate that a different kind of enquiry is possible and necessary to answer them.

So far it has been suggested that the history of political thought is one form of enquiry but that there is no reason to think it exhausts the questions in which the political theorist is interested. Another kind of enquiry is that identified here as social theory, which is concerned to develop a general empirical explanation of social institutions and practices, including the political. Marx, Durkheim and Weber are obvious examples of thinkers who were primarily social theorists in this sense.[3] All were concerned to try to develop explanatory theories of a broadly empirical kind open to testing by historical and sociological evidence. The borderline between social theory and history is at best blurred and some would deny any distinction at all, but it is perhaps possible to detect at least a significant difference of emphasis. Whereas social theory is concerned to develop general theories and to understand particular events as instances of general types, revolutions for example, history is more usually concerned with the particularity of historical events, this or that revolution. The difference between social theory and political philosophy is in the former's claim to be at least in principle empirically testable.

3

What then of political philosophy? There are two aspects here, both in need of some discussion, though I shall have more to say about one than the other. The first concerns the *philosophical* character of political philosophy and what this might mean I shall explore a little later. Secondly, political philosophy is philosophy which takes *politics* as its subject matter and it is with this I shall begin, though it will not be treated at all thoroughly. The nature of the political is an obscure and difficult issue, and I have no startling or original definition of it to offer, though perhaps in the context of the present volume that is not all to the bad. However, some sense of what a subject is 'about' is both necessary and unavoidable; and it is sometimes useful to attempt to articulate that sense in a reasonably coherent and self-conscious manner. It may be, though, that there are no convincing reasons in favour of

[3] See for a good account of their work and the character of social theory A. Giddens, *Capitalism and Modern Social Theory* (Cambridge, 1971).

choosing one conception of politics rather than another. My own preference is for a narrowish conception of politics, and some reasons are offered for this but they amount to something considerably less than a convincing justification. Indeed it is very doubtful that they would persuade those who disagree that they were wrong to disagree. Furthermore, it is not always clear quite what hangs on different conceptions of politics, for even those who favour a narrow conception might agree that explanations of politics often involve the non-political. Thus in practical terms the study of politics might not proceed very differently despite differences about what 'politics' is.

It is possible to distinguish two tendencies within definitions of politics. The first emphasizes that politics is a specific and limited class of human activities. On this view a debate in Parliament, an election, the activities of pressure groups and the enactment of legislation might be thought of as clear examples of politics. On the other hand, a husband and wife arguing about who should cook the dinner, the teaching of mathematics, the performance of a Mozart symphony and the act of making love are not politics, though in some circumstances all may be influenced by or have consequences for politics. The second tendency is inclined to reject the view that there is only a specific and limited class of activities which can be identified as political. It tends to see politics everywhere, as at least an aspect or dimension of all or most significant human activities. (Indeed on extreme versions of this view, politics is not even a specifically human activity, but one shared with at least some part of the animal kingdom.) The argument between the husband and wife, the teaching of mathematics, the performance of a Mozart symphony and making love might all on this view be understood as political. Characteristically, accounts of politics in which 'government' or 'legislation' are central are examples of the first tendency, while those which understand politics as 'social interaction' or 'anything to do with the production, distribution and use of resources' would be examples of the second. These tendencies within the definition of politics are matters of degree rather than kind, but in some cases the degree of difference is very great indeed.

My own view of politics is to be located firmly within the first tendency. It holds that politics is a particular activity associated with the government of a community, and is perhaps very close to the famous account of politics offered by Michael Oakeshott who writes:

> Politics I take to be the activity of attending to the general arrangements
> of a set of people whom chance or choice have brought together. In this
> sense, families, clubs and learned societies have their 'politics'. But the
> communities in which this manner of activity is pre-eminent are the
> hereditary co-operative groups, many of them of ancient lineage, all of
> them aware of a past, a present and a future, which we call 'states'.[4]

Politics, as it is understood here, is principally those activities by which
the members of a group formally regulate their relations with each
other, and particularly in that most extensive and inclusive of groups,
the state. The special character of the state lies in its being a compulsory,
coercive association. It is, in theory at least, the supreme regulator
within a given territory. Politics is paradigmatically concerned with
government and legislation; the deliberating, deciding and implementing of the rules by which a state conducts its affairs. Other groups
characteristically lack the self-authenticating, compulsory quality of the
state, though they may share sufficient similarities that reference to their
'politics' is natural enough. Cricket clubs, businesses, perhaps even
families and groups of states sometimes need rules and regulations for
the conduct of their affairs. Individuals need to live with each other in
organizations and institutions smaller than states, and states need to
coexist in some kind of ordered relationship with each other.

The conception of politics that has been briefly elaborated here is
moderately restrictive but even so is difficult to delimit in any very clear
way. There are, however, obvious dangers in the endless extension of
the term politics so that it seems to include within it all significant
human activities. In particular, if politics becomes coterminous with all
significant human activity, then any specific sense of politics is likely to
be lost. It is an elementary point, but one which needs to be made in this
context, that characterizations of activity derive their sense from their
distinctness from other characterizations, and the broader and more
inclusive they are the greater the danger of them being at best flaccidly
general and at worst superfluous or redundant. However, none of this
is intended to deny that unusual or idiosyncratic accounts of politics
may often have something to teach us. They may make connections not
previously thought of or reveal distinctions where none are normally
perceived, but each such account has to be judged on its own merits and

---

[4] M. Oakeshott, 'Political Education', in Michael Oakeshott, *Rationalism in Politics and Other
Essays* (London, 1962), p. 112.

everything will depend upon the details, their context and their point. Such accounts can be illuminating and perceptive but they can also be myopic and perverse.

4

So far the question at issue has been the nature of politics and some account of it has been tentatively offered. However, the problem to which the bulk of the remainder of this chapter will be devoted is a characterization and evaluation of what is distinctively *philosophical* about political philosophy. In short, what specifically can philosophy contribute to an understanding of politics? However, rather than confronting this question directly the most productive way of approaching some of the issues involved is to do so more obliquely through a brief summary of the recent history of political philosophy in the English-speaking world. [5]

A particularly good place to begin is with the now celebrated pronouncement of Peter Laslett, who in 1956 declared that 'for the moment, anyway, political philosophy is dead'. [6] This claim, despite a pardonable degree of rhetorical exaggeration, contained a good deal of truth in that it reflected the extremely barren condition of political philosophy at the time. There seemed to be a widespread conviction that political philosophy, at least as anything recognizably connected with the great texts, had come to an end sometime in the nineteenth century, though precisely when this end occurred and what its causes were were subject to some disagreement. There were those who saw Hegel as a watershed in this process, though often for different reasons. A few saw in Hegel's work the summit of political philosophy, while rather more regarded it as a nadir, in which political philosophy was exposed as bogus and brought into disrepute by obscure, pretentious, Teutonic jargon. Others championed Marx as having inflicted the death-blows to political philsophy through his repudiation of abstract speculation for the concrete science of historical materialism. Still others, less impressed

---

[5] The account of political philosophy which follows is exclusively concerned with the developments in Britain and the United States. The history of political philosophy in Europe is very different but for reasons of space cannot be discussed here.

[6] P. Laslett, 'Introduction' to P. Laslett (ed.), *Philosophy, Politics and Society*, first series (Oxford, 1956), p. vii.

with the specific contribution of Marx, looked to the scientific temper of the age, the gradually emergent social sciences, for a displacement of philosophy by political science. It was conceded by all that there had been no sharp break and that political philosophy had limped lamely into the twentieth century, but mainly in works such as Bosanquet's *The Philosophical Theory of the State*, which had the air of being philosophical fossils. However, there had been long gaps between the emergence of important theorists in the history of political philosophy previously and the question remains of what might have led to the conviction in the middle of the twentieth century that this was not a passing phase, and that the condition of political philosophy might be terminal.

Probably the most important reason had to do with developments within philosophy in the first half of this century. In particular the emergence of an aggressive positivism followed by a narrow and restrictive conception of philosophy as 'linguistic analysis' seemed to have little room for serious political philosophy. Positivism was particularly radical, especially in an extreme form, such as the logical positivism of A. J. Ayers's *Language, Truth and Logic*, for it seemed to deny any place at all for political philosophy. If the only meaningful statements were either empirical hypotheses, which were the business of science, or tautologies, statements true by definition, which insofar as they were of any interest were the province of logic, there seemed to be nothing left to constitute the subjects of aesthetics, ethics or political philosophy. Most political philosophy on this view was no more than a declaration of preferences or the expression of attitudes, and that which was not was properly the business of an empirically rigorous social science. Logical positivism of this form, however, soon ran into difficulties, which cannot be entered into here, but it did leave a substantial legacy. In particular, its scientism had an important effect on the development of political science, most notably in the United States, where there was a widespread and self-conscious move to displace political philosophy with a study modelled upon the natural sciences. Furthermore, the linguistic philosophy which superseded logical positivism and was influenced by it was only marginally more receptive to political philosophy. It did not deny the possibility of political philosophy, but its reduction of philosophy to an examination of the ordinary use of words seemed to drain it of all imagination, creativity and significance. Probably the best example of this tendency is T. D.

Weldon's *The Vocabulary of Politics* in which all political disagreements are seen as resting on verbal confusions or to be matters for empirical investigation. There is virtually no sense of there being anything serious involved in political philosophy, which seems to be limited entirely to sorting out purely verbal confusions.

The overall impact of philosophical developments in the decades before the mid-fifties was to restrict and trivialize political philosophy. This tendency was brought into even sharper relief by the enormous horror of political events in the period from the Great War and culminating in the Nazi concentration camps. This constituted a second important inhibiting influence on political philosophy. The meaningless deaths of millions in the extermination camps of one of the most culturally and philosophically sophisticated countries of Europe seemed to leave political philosophy mute and in a condition of hopeless ineffectiveness. The problems of seriousness of purpose and appropriateness of tone appeared impossible to resolve in a context where political events had an almost unimaginable awesomeness, and yet philosophical developments had so radically diminished the ambitions and resources of political philosophy. The result was the period from the forties to the early sixties when political philosophy seemed at best barren and at worst non-existent. It was indeed a case of 'whereof one cannot speak, thereof one must be silent'. However, the sixties began to see a significant revitalization of political philosophy marked by increasing activity and a return to a much bolder conception of its legitimate concerns.

The claim that there has been a significant revival in the fortunes of political philosophy is easily justified. Any survey of journals and publishers' lists would reveal the increased activity. However, decisive confirmation of this transformation was probably the publication in 1972 of John Rawls's massive and monumental *A Theory of Justice*, received to almost universal critical acclaim as a masterpiece, fully in the tradition of the great texts of political philosophy. Furthermore it has spawned an enormous literature of such proportions that even only a decade after its publication it is probably nearly a lifetime's work to read all that has been written about it or inspired by it. Furthermore, it has been followed by a number of major works of political philosophy and an extraordinary plethora of papers, books and even new journals, of which *Philosophy and Public Affairs* is generally considered the most distinguished though it was first published the year before Rawls' book. This work has shown an increasing confidence in its ability to discuss issues of practical political importance and relevance, such as the justification of war, human rights, civil disobedience, social inequality and much else. It certainly seems that political philosophy has performed the Lazarus-like accomplishment that Laslett's peculiar language had allowed as an unlikely possibility.

The explanation of this resurgence of political philosophy is less clear than the reasons for its decline, though undoubtedly both philosophical and political developments were again important. The Nazi holocaust was no longer part of the direct political experience of younger political philosophers. More significantly, there was the erosion of the extreme 'cold war' mentality, the counter-cultural explosion of the sixties and most important of all perhaps the fierce political controversy occasioned by the war in Vietnam, all of which decisively refuted the thesis that western societies had experienced 'the end of ideology'. Philosophically the heyday of linguistic philosophy was past and the locus of philosophical innovation had shifted across the Atlantic from Oxford to the Ivy League colleges. The view of philosophy as concerned with linguistic puzzles arising from lack of attention to the minutiae of ordinary language was gradually superseded by a restoration of a more traditional conception of philosophy as concerned with genuine problems, and of the proper methods of philosophy not as a detailed analysis of ordinary language but the formulation of philosophical theories supported by abstract arguments. While the political climate of the sixties proved in some respects short-lived, it probably provided a crucial initial impetus while the less spectacular developments within philosophy have proved more durable and hence helped to sustain a more ambitious conception of political philosophy.

5

This thumbnail sketch of the recent history of political philosophy is of course something of a caricature, and perhaps a familiar one at that, but its broad contours seem reasonably uncontroversial. However, the story has been presented in this way partly because I wish to challenge it. It is not the narrative of events nor their explanation with which I shall take issue but its sanguine tone; its optimistic, perhaps even self-congratulatory character as the success story of political philosophy. Do these developments represent quite the triumph for political philosophy which they purport to be? In particular I shall question what is perhaps the single most significant feature of this development which is the whole-hearted embracing of a normative or recommendatory role for political philosophy and the comparative neglect or even rejection of what I shall call, for want of a better term, 'conceptual analysis'. Both these central terms need to be explained more fully. By normative or recommendatory political philosophy I mean that which aims to advance and defend particular political proposals, to recommend specific political values or even ideologies. By conceptual analysis, and it is important to distinguish this from what was earlier called 'linguistic philosophy', I do not mean a kind of lexicography or summary of the ordinary uses of particular words, but rather the eludication and exploration of *concepts* central to political life and discourse, such as power, authority, sovereignty, freedom, equality and rights among others. The elucidation and exploration of concepts is not a concern for mere words, for different words can be used to express the same concept, as in any dictionary, and the same word can be used in different sense to mark different concepts. Of course the enquiry into the meaning of concepts must begin with the way language is used but nothing said here implies for example that there is only one 'correct' use of political concepts.

Conceptual analysis involves articulating the meaning of concepts, their presuppositions and interrelationships and exploring their internal coherence and consistency. Political philosophy understood as conceptual analysis in this way is the attempt to make explicit the meaning, assumptions and implications of the language we use to make sense of political activity and ideas. However, it is also indirectly critical, for it may discover assumptions which when made explicit can be seen to be implausible or unrealistic, implications which seem unattractive or obscure, or, even more dramatically, inconsistency and incoherence at the heart of some understandings of political concepts. More positively, besides producing greater self-consciousness and clarity in the understanding of political ideas and activity, a virtue it seems currently fashionable to underrate, it may enlarge our appreciation of a variety of political ideas and ideologies. This is, I think, a rather larger and bolder account of what 'conceptual analysis' may involve than is usual. Furthermore, while preserving claims to be an authentic enquiry capable of producing objective conclusions, it does not deny that conceptual analysis can be genuinely critical and even profoundly illuminating. If it uncovers confusions they are unlikely, in many cases, to be merely verbal confusions but rather to be deeply rooted in thinking about politics. It may also reveal that the apparently confused is much more coherent and consistent than it appears. In all these respects political philosophy conceived as conceptual analysis is a particularly rewarding and revealing enquiry, and it is this that is being defended here, and not the overly narrow and attenuated conception dominant in the fifties and associated with 'linguistic' or 'Oxford' philosophy.

Much recent work in political philosophy has, however, as mentioned earlier, either rejected or downgraded conceptual analysis, though perhaps not in the precise form adumbrated here. Rawls again provides a good example of this tendency, for, as his title suggests, *A Theory of Justice* is concerned not with any analysis of the concept of justice but with the elaboration and defence of a substantive moral point of view. As Rawls himself writes, he wants 'to leave questions of meaning and definition aside and to get on with the task of developing a substantive theory of justice'.[7] Throughout there is an impatience with questions of meaning and definition which is shared by much contemporary work in political philosophy. Despite the book's length and extensive discussion of methodology, Rawls himself makes little attempt to offer a serious critique of conceptual analysis, but among the charges that others have levelled at it there are perhaps three which are persistent and recurring. These charges, which are not wholly consistent with each other, are that conceptual analysis is trivial or at least unduly restrictive; that it is necessarily conservative; and that it is impossible.[8] I shall briefly consider each of these criticisms, concluding that none of them represents an entirely persuasive objection to conceptual analysis as it has been characterized here. In dealing with these criticisms, this characterization of conceptual analysis will be filled out in a little more detail.

The first criticism is that which I have to some extent endorsed when applied to the linguistic philosophy of the fifties but which is much less

---

[7]   John Rawls, *A Theory of Justice* (Oxford, 1972), p. 579.
[8]   Some of the criticisms are discussed in A. Wertheimer, 'Is Ordinary Language Analysis Conservative?', *Political Theory* 4 (1976). Also relevant is D. Miller, 'Linguistic Philosophy and Political Theory', in D. Miller and L. Siedentop (eds), *The Nature of Political Theory* (Oxford, 1983).

persuasive when directed at the enlarged and richer account of conceptual analysis advocated here. It is, though, sometimes maintained that conceptual analysis is an abdication of the responsibility and promise of political philosophy to attempt to discover the best form of polity or to teach persons how they should live together. However, this is a line of thought that can be turned back on the objector, for it merely assumes that political philosophy is capable, in principle at least, of offering some demonstration or conclusive arguments which will resolve the normative disagreements which are the stuff of so much of political life and thought. But what is the basis of this assumption, and how on this view is political philosophy as a serious academic enquiry to be distinguished from the activities of ideologists, propagandists and pamphleteers? These are more serious and important questions than the amount of attention they have received from enthusiasts for a strongly normative conception of political philosophy would suggest. It is undoubtedly true that most of the 'great texts' do engage in strong normative recommendation, though they do much else besides, but this does not settle the argument. They also engaged in *a priori* sociology and speculative historical conjectures, which would be rejected today as unsociological and unhistorical. Thus it is not possible simply and uncritically to take the 'great texts' as the models of political philosophy any more than they can be taken as models of sociology or history, though this is not to deny that they contain a great deal of political philosophy and much of it of a very high order.

The issue at stake in the charge that conceptual analysis is trivial or too narrow is the proper scope of political philosophy. Rawls likens the 'theories' of moral and political philosophy to those of the natural sciences, but he applies this analogy very inaccurately. Strictly applied, the question to be asked would be whether there is any more reason to think that political philosophy is capable of adjudicating between political values and viewpoints than the philosophy of science or epistemology between competing scientific theories? What needs to be shown if these more ambitious aspirations for political philosophy are to be taken seriously is how it is possible for it to show for example that socialism is morally superior to capitalism or vice versa; or that equality is a more important political value than freedom or the reverse; or to demonstrate that war can or cannot be justified in particular circumstances. Furthermore, the aspirations of conceptual analysis need no apology, for the understanding of the central concepts of political analysis and argument is hardly trivial. However, whereas the view of political philosophy as essentially recommendatory or normative collapses any distinction between political and philosophical interests and argument, it is essential to conceptual analysis that some such distinction between political argument and the philosophical analysis of political argument be preserved.

At this point in the discussion the first criticism of conceptual analysis often slips into the third criticism. The argument tends to move from the claim that conceptual analysis is trivial to the claim that it is impossible. So this will be discussed further in conjunction with that criticism, but, before doing so, the criticism that conceptual analysis is essentially conservative will be considered. The substance of this criticism is that both in its practical consequences and in its conception of philosophical method, conceptual analysis tends to be supportive of the established political order. However, when examined carefully, it is not at all clear that there is really much to be said for this objection. Conceptual analysis need not display a prejudice in favour of any particular political outlook, whether radical, liberal or conservative. If the case of Gerald MacCallum's analysis of liberty as a triadic relationship is taken as an example, it is not at all clear, whatever its merits or defects, that it can legitimately be charged with being politically conservative. According to MacCallum's analysis, the freedom of some individual or group

> is always freedom from some constraint or restriction on, interference with, or barrier to doing, not doing, becoming or not becoming, something. Such freedom is thus always *of* something (an agent or agents), *from* something, *to* do, not do, become or not become something; it is a triadic relation. Taking the format 'x is (is not) free from y to do (not do, become, not become) z', x ranges over agents, y ranges over such 'preventing conditions' as constraints, restrictions, interferences, and barriers, and z ranges over actions or conditions of character or circumstance.[9]

There exists in MacCallum's analysis the beginnings of an understanding of freedom which will facilitate the identification of both points of agreement and disagreement between the varying conceptions to be found in political debate and discussion.

[9] G. C. MacCallum, 'Negative and Positive Freedom', in A. de Crespigny and A. Wertheimer (eds), *Contemporary Political Theory* (London, 1970), p. 109.

The example from MacCallum is a fairly elementary one and it is not being suggested that there are no objections which could be made to it. However, it is not at all clear how such an analysis can be regarded as politically conservative or providing tacit support for the *status quo*. Conceptual analysis is an enquiry into the terms of political discourse but what this enquiry will reveal, as with all genuine enquiries, is an open question until the enquiry has been undertaken. It may reveal deep incoherences, ambiguities, dubious presuppositions of concepts deployed in conservative political discourse, but then again, it may not. Both remain possibilities. It is true that conceptual analysis is in general concerned with concepts which are actually deployed, but this concern is entirely anodyne in that it includes 'radical' and 'left-wing' discourse as well as 'conservative' or 'reactionary'. The concept of 'repressive tolerance' for example may be as interesting to this kind of political philosopher as to Marcuse, though whether it will be found to be coherent and intelligible will depend upon the results of an enquiry. It is arguable that it is not conceptual analysis which is politically partisan, but rather the conception of political philosophy as normative or recommendatory which lacks the appropriate objectivity. It is very often the case that such political 'philosophizing', rather than following the argument wherever it leads, largely consists of *post hoc* rationalizations of preconceived political commitments.

The third criticism of conceptual analysis, and the most difficult to deal with briefly, is the claim that it is an impossible enterprise. This may appear a curious contention in that there seem to be many examples of what is alleged to be impossible, but the criticism cannot be refuted so easily, merely by reference to apparent counter-examples, for whether they *are* counter-examples is just the issue in question. The core of this objection, which in some respects combines the two previous criticisms but pushes them much further, is that the claim of conceptual analysis to be a genuine academic enquiry distinct from political argument is bogus. Thus, according to this argument, political philosophy cannot be separated from political engagement and the mistake of the proponents of conceptual analysis is to think that it can. This is an issue of obviously crucial importance and not one that will be resolved here. However, it is worth considering the implications of this criticism, for, if it is valid, then it seriously undermines the claims of political philosophy to be a genuine enquiry properly to be found in academic institutions. For, if political philosophy is not significantly different from the kind of political argument to be found in bar-rooms, common-rooms or hustings, then there is a legitimate question to be asked about its place in a university at all. Of course there is a place for political debate and discussion, even within a university, but is that place on the syllabus of a university department?

The problem of the relationship between political philosophy and ordinary political discourse is a complex one. Clearly there must be some relationship, for at the very least the latter affords the subject matter of the former. Furthermore the view that political philosophy cannot have implications for practical politics is simply untenable. [10] On the other hand, an account of political philosophy which sees it as directly engaged in the advocacy or recommendation of preferred political principles threatens to reduce it to the level of a handmaiden to ideology. However, the account of political philosophy elucidated here does not pretend that conceptual analysis has no implications for practical politics, but it suggests that those implications will be indirect and the result of disinterested enquiry. If political philosophy shows some uses of political concepts to be incoherent, mutually inconsistent or based upon presuppositions which when revealed are unattractive, then for anyone who takes their political ideas and engagements seriously these results will occasion a reconsideration and response. Of course, though political philosophy can reveal these features of some uses of political concepts, it cannot ensure that they will be taken into account by political activists. Furthermore, the 'conclusions' of political philosophy may themselves be subject to dispute and disagreement, and anyway are only the best available at a given time which further enquiry may modify or overturn. However, these are the conditions of all enquiries, historical, scientific or logical, and political philosophy is not exempt from them. The task of political philosophy is the critical examination of the concepts and beliefs in terms of which the political is understood. It does not possess the resources for instructing as to what is right in politics, but it does provide the resources for exploring the internal coherence, presuppositions and logical implications of political beliefs and practices.

[10] Such a case has been argued, unsuccessfully I think, in G. Graham, 'Practical Politics and Philosophical Inquiry', *The Philosophical Quarterly* 28 (1978). See also the criticism of J. Liddington, 'Graham on Politics and Philosophy', a reply by Graham, and further criticisms in D. Hall and T. Modood, 'Practical Politics and Philosophical Inquiry: A Note', all in *The Philosophical Quarterly* 29 (1979). A very useful discussion of these issues is P. P. Nicholson, 'The Relationship Between Political Theory and Political Practice', *Political Studies* 21 (1973).

6

The value of political philosophy so conceived to the student of politics is, I hope, obvious. There is a genuine enquiry to engage the student; it can be done well or badly; and it can produce conclusions which increase the understanding of politics and may have indirect practical relevance. In short, political philosophy is an important element in the process of trying to make sense of political ideas and practices and their relationship to the larger life of which they are a part. To invert the intention of a famous remark of Marx, the point of political philosophy is not to change the world but to understand it. However, in trying to understand it, political philosophy may indirectly contribute to its change. Furthermore, both the ambitions and methods of conceptual analysis, as it has been interpreted here, are sufficiently shared by the 'great texts' for this enterprise to deserve the title of political philosophy. Of course political philosophy does not exhaust the study of politics but no study which excludes it can claim to be exhaustive.

7

Marxism and politics

ALEX CALLINICOS

1

What is politics? The answer given to this question by Marxism is so radical as to disqualify it from being merely another 'approach' to the study of politics. Marxism (throughout this essay I shall use the term as shorthand for what has come to be known as the classical Marxism of Marx and Engels, Lenin and Trotsky, Luxemburg and Gramsci[1]) denies that politics is a persisting feature of every form of society. Furthermore, it claims that politics, where it does exist, cannot be studied in isolation from the rest of society. Finally, Marxism, insofar as it is a practical programme as well as a body of theoretical analysis, seeks the *abolition* of politics. These claims are obviously incompatible with the notion of an autonomous discipline of Politics.

2

To appreciate the force of the Marxist view of politics, it may be helpful to consider first more conventional approaches. It is customary to look on politics as arising from and concerned with a set of formal political institutions – in our own society, Parliament, Cabinet, elections and so forth. It is assumed that these institutions are relatively autonomous of the rest of social life. Politics is thus seen as abstracted from the social whole.

The discipline of Politics tends to reflect this view. Thus, political theory seeks to settle such questions as the nature of the just society and

[1] See J. Molyneux, 'What is the Real Marxist Tradition?', *International Socialism* 2:20 (1983).

the rights and duties of the citizens. The methods it uses are those of conceptual analysis and *a priori* reflection on first principles. The underlying assumption is that there is a set of political problems so universal as to be common to every form of society, which political theory can resolve without empirical investigation of the specific features of any particular society. Notoriously, this has led political thinkers again and again to treat the peculiar problems of their own time and place as problems for *any* society.

Political Science focuses upon political institutions. It seeks to un-cover the distribution of power within actual political systems. But this enquiry proceeds without any coherent attempt to relate the distribution of political power to wider patterns of social and economic inequality. Social forces figure only as they impinge on these institutions from outside, as in the case of pressure groups. The boom subject of electoral behaviour studies obsessively catalogues citizens' political preferences. Its attempts to relate, for example, the phenomenon of 'partisan de-alignment' in Britain to the social, economic and political crises of the past twenty years are, however, superficial and perfunctory.

Marxism challenges the basic assumption behind the discipline of Politics, namely that there is a permanent and autonomous feature of society called politics. In the first place, in the realist tradition of Machiavelli and Hobbes, Marxism insists that politics is not concerned so much with rights as with *power*. 'Starting with Machiavelli, Hobbes, Spinoza, Bodinus and others of modern times,' Marx wrote approvingly, 'might has been represented as the basis of right . . . . if power is taken as the basis of right . . . then right, law, etc., are merely the symptom, the expression of *other* relations upon which state power rest.'[2]

Marx thus declared his lack of sympathy for political theory as it is practised today. The task of theory is not to find a moral or juridical justification for the exercise of political power, but to understand the social processes which generate and sustain political institutions and practices. Any sharp distinction between political *theory* and Political *Science*, between *a priori* theorizing and empirical investigation, is rejected. The study of politics proceeds in the manner of other sciences, through the discovery of causal patterns.

---

[2] K. Marx and F. Engels, *Collected Works* (50 vols., London, 1975 –) (hereinafter cited as *CW*) V, p. 322 and 329.

By the same token, no science simply observes the world, without any assumptions about what it is likely to discover. The role of theory is to lay down guidelines for empirical enquiry, suggesting the directions in which research is likely to be fruitful.[3] Thus, Marxism denies that politics can be studied in isolation from the rest of society. Its object is what Marx called 'the ensemble of the social relations'.[4] Society can thus only be understood as a structured whole, a totality. The different forms of social life, including politics, are comprehensible as aspects of this whole. It is its role within the social totality which determines the nature of politics.

As I have already noted, such an approach undermines the very concept of a separate discipline of Politics. Political behaviour, if Marxism is right, can only be studied with the help of a variety of disciplines – Economics, Sociology, Anthropology, History, and so on. Indeed, one could go further and say that, according to Marxism, there is only one social science, which embraces and integrates all these supposedly distinct disciplines. The name Marxists usually give to this unified science is historical materialism, the systematic study of social formations founded by Marx. Such a view of social science does not rule out the possibility of specializing in particular areas, but it does suggest that every limited study should constantly seek to place its researches in the context of the social whole.

The strength of such a holist approach to the study of society is that it challenges the fragmentation of the existing social sciences. The attempt to carve out distinct disciplines leads to the creation of artificial divisions. It is impossible to understand contemporary British politics without a deep acquaintance with the country's economic and social history, but this immediately means crossing the boundaries of Politics into Economics, Sociology and History. The same strictures apply to the other would-be social sciences. The attempt to reduce Economics to a body of mathematical techniques lacking any relation to the study of social and political forces has made its contribution to the disasters of monetarism.

3

From a Marxist point of view, then, politics must be viewed as merely one aspect of the social whole, to be studied as part of an integrated

[3] See I. Lakatos, *Philosophical Papers* (Cambridge, 1978).
[4] *CW*, V, p. 4.

analysis of that totality. More specifically, in Lenin's words, 'politics is the most concentrated expression of economics.'[5] Political institutions and struggles arise from, and can only be understood in the light of, the basic conflicts of the social whole. These conflicts are generated at the level of what Marx called the forces and relations of production.

Marx's view of the social whole was most succinctly expressed in these famous lines written in 1859:

> In the social production of their life, men enter into definite relations that are indispensable and independent of their will, relations of production which correspond to a definite stage of development of their material productive forces. The sum total of these relations of production constitutes the economic structure of society, the real foundation, on which rises a legal and political superstructure and to which correspond definite forms of social consciousness. The mode of production of material life conditions the social, political and intellectual life-process in general. It is not the consciousness of men that determines their being, but, on the contrary, their social being that determines their consciousness.[6]

Production is thus the 'real foundation' of social life. Politics, law and culture all arise upon its basis. But production itself has two aspects, the material and the social. The material aspect is what Marx calls *the forces of production*. These correspond roughly to what we today call technology. The instruments which we use in order to produce things, whether they be the cave-dweller's flint or the robots in modern car-plants, and the physical strength, skill and knowledge used to set these instruments in motion, make up the productive forces of humanity. At its most basic, history is the record of human beings' increasingly more sophisticated abilities to produce. This process is what Marx described as the development of the productive forces.

Unfortunately, that is not the end of the story:

> In production, men enter into relation not only with nature. They produce only by co-operating in a certain way and mutually exchanging their activities. In order to produce, they enter into definite connections and relations with one another and only within these social connections and relations does their relation with nature, does production, take place.[7]

[5] V. I. Lenin, *Collected Works* (Moscow, 1965), XXXII, p. 32.
[6] K. Marx and F. Engels, *Selected Works* (3 vols., Moscow, 1973) (hereinafter cited as *SW*) I, p. 503.
[7] *CW*, IX, p. 211.

These *social relations of production* have given rise in the past few thousand years to the division of society into classes. A minority is able to gain control of the means of production, that is, of the land, and of the instruments of production. They use this control to force the direct producers, the mass of the population who do the actual work of producing society's wealth, to perform surplus-labour. In other words, the direct producer, whether he or she be a slave, a peasant, or a modern wage-labourer, is compelled to work, not only to meet his or her own needs, and those of any dependants he or she may have, but also to meet the needs (including those for luxuries and the means of waging war) of the owner of the means of production, whether he be a slave-master, a feudal lord or a capitalist. 'What distinguishes the various economic formations of society . . . is the form in which this surplus-labour is in each case extorted from the immediate producer, the worker.'[8]

Such a view of class society places exploitation, the extraction of surplus-labour, at its heart. 'Class', writes the ancient historian G. E. M. de Ste Croix, 'is essentially the way in which exploitation is reflected in a social structure.'[9] Marx's *Capital* is above all a demonstration of the way in which capitalism is founded upon exploitation. The source of the profits on which capitalism as an economic system depends is the surplus-value extracted from workers within production. Capitalism is but the latest form of class society.

4

What implications does this analysis of society have for the study of politics? In the first place, politics can only be understood in the context of a process of historical change. Marx's account of the forces and relations of production is a *dynamic* one. The two come into conflict with one another, and, as they do so, social formations are compelled to undergo change: 'The social relations within which individuals produce, *the social relations of production, change, are transformed, with the change and development of the material means of production, the productive forces.*'[10]

This conflict between the forces and relations of production finds

[8]   K. Marx, *Capital* I (Harmondsworth, 1976), p. 325.
[9]   G. E. M. de Ste Croix, *The Class Struggle in the Ancient Greek World* (London, 1981), p. 51.
[10]   *CW*, IX, p. 212.

expression in the struggle between classes. The exploitive relations of production which form the basis of every class society compel the exploited class to resist. Exploitation thus gives rise to class struggle, the constant battle between exploiter and exploited. The opening sentence of the *Communist Manifesto* declares: 'The history of all hitherto existing society is the history of class struggle.'[11] This class struggle is 'the immediate driving power of history'.[12]

It is exploitation and the class struggle which provide the key to any genuine understanding of politics:

> The specific economic form in which unpaid surplus-labour is pumped out of the direct producers, determines the relationship of rulers and ruled . . . . It is always the direct relationship of the owners of the conditions of production to the direct producers . . . which reveals the innermost secret, the hidden basis of the entire social structure, and with it . . . the corresponding specific form of the state.[13]

Politics must always be traced back to its 'hidden basis' in the class struggle. Marx observed this injunction himself most successfully in his writings on France, which include such masterpieces of historico-political analysis as *The Eighteenth Brumaire of Louis Bonaparte*. But more than that, precisely because politics arise from the class struggle, it is an historically transient phenomenon.

To see why the existence of politics is coterminous with that of classes let us consider some of the rival definitions of politics. One such definition, proffered by Albert Weale in chapter 3, is that of politics as a process of collective choice, as an activity in which individuals combine to make some decision. But such a definition does not demarcate politics, as it is conventionally understood at any rate, from other processes of collective choice. Weale does not claim otherwise: he simply suggests that conceiving politics as collective choice will illuminate some of its distinctive problems. There are, however, features of politics other than decision-making. One, the existence of conflicts of interest between individuals or groups, can be brought within the scope of Weale's definition. A second, force or coercion, cannot, and Peter Nicholson in chapter 2 suggests that it is force that

[11]   Ibid., VI, p. 483.
[12]   *SW*, III, p. 94.
[13]   K. Marx, *Capital* III (Moscow, 1971), p. 791.

distinguishes politics as a social activity. Conceiving politics as coercion starkly highlights a third issue, the inequalities of power between different individuals and groups.

5

These three issues – conflict, force and power – focus upon a fourth, the state. For it is on the institutions of state power that, as Graeme Moodie emphasizes (see chapter 1), the process of political decision-making centres. Furthermore, the state is, ultimately, a coercive institution, according to Max Weber's classic definition, depending upon the monopoly of legitimate force in a particular territory. And the conflicts between different groups tend to revolve around the objective of seizing, or influencing the exercise of, state power.

Politics is thus inextricably associated with the existence of states. But if the state is conceived as a specialized apparatus of coercion, involving the existence of what Lenin called 'special bodies of armed men' (standing armies, police forces, etc.), then it is, like classes, a comparatively recent phenomenon in the history of human societies. Indeed, so Marxists argue, and there is much anthropological and historical evidence to support them, the formation of states is part of the same process as that in which society is divided into classes.

'The state', Engels wrote in his classic essay *The Origins of the Family, Private Property and the State*, 'is a product of society at a certain stage of development; it is the admission that this society has become entangled in an impossible contradiction with itself, that it is split into irreconcilable antagonisms which it is powerless to dispel.'[14] The emergence of class exploitation means that it is no longer possible, as was the case in pre-class societies, for all (male) members of society to bear arms. The preservation of class domination requires 'the establishment of a *public power* which no longer directly coincides with the population organizing itself as an armed force . . . . This public power exists in every state; it consists not merely of armed men but also of material adjuncts, prisons and institutions of coercion of all kinds.'[15] Different states are simply different forms of class domination: 'Political

[14] *SW*, III, pp. 326–7.
[15] Ibid., p. 327. For a discussion of contemporary archaeological evidence supportive of Engels's arguments, see R. Carneiro, 'A Theory of the Origin of the State,' *Science* 169 (1970).

power, properly so called, is merely the organised power of one class for oppressing another.'[16]

Such a view of politics does not involve the naive and Utopian belief that it is only in class societies that coercion is to be found. There is plenty of evidence of violence within and between 'primitive' pre-class societies. *Any* society may need to resort to force where individuals will not observe the decisions that have been collectively arrived at. But 'coercion' takes on a different order of meaning where there exist specialized apparatuses separate from the mass of the population and monopolizing the legitimate use of force. The central Marxist thesis with respect to politics is that state societies are also class societies; or rather, they are state societies *because* they are class societies.

It follows that there are no universal 'political problems'. Adrian Leftwich suggests, for example (see chapter 4), that politics exists wherever human beings take decisions concerning the use and distribution of resources. The implication is that politics is to be found in every society, and that it exists at the micro level of families and communities as well as at the macro level of state institutions. Such a view of politics is very different from that taken by Marxism.

First, by tracing politics to the decisions every society must take about the use and distribution of resources, Leftwich offers a model of social action rather similar to that provided by neo-classical economics. In the latter, human subjects are treated as rational economic agents guided by the motive of maximizing their utilities irrespective of their specific situation in question. The objection which Marxism has always made to this model is that people's interests will vary according to their position in the social relations of production. In class societies, their interests will be antagonistic, because they will be generated by a structure of class exploitation. The course of action which will be rational for an individual to take faced with the eternal problems of the use and distribution of resources will depend upon his or her class-specific interests. It will also depend on the individual's power to achieve his or her wants, and this in turn is, once again, largely conditioned by the class position occupied by that individual. Any study of a society's decision-making processes must start with an appraisal of the structure of the forces and relations of production prevailing in that society.

[16]   *CW*, VI, p. 505.

More specifically, Leftwich's view of politics suggests that it exists in non-state societies in a sense analogous to the manner in which it does in state societies. The danger with such a general definition is that it makes politics an essentially benign process. The decisions taken by hunter-gatherer societies and by families, neither of which are characterized by class antagonism or state coercion, are treated as the same kind of activity as politics in class societies, in which both predominate. The brute facts of inequality, coercion and power that preoccupied the great political theorists from Plato and Aristotle to Hegel and Marx are wiped out of the picture.

Moreover, a focus on the 'micropolitics' of families and communities can be equally misleading. As we have already seen, Marxism insists on placing politics in the context of the social whole. Nevertheless, it is the institutions of state power which are the focus of political struggle. Marx wrote of the 'concentration of bourgeois society in the form of the state'.[17] More recently, Nicos Poulantzas has expressed the same thought by calling the state 'the *specific materialized condensation* of a relationship of forces among classes'.[18] In other words, while the state is not autonomous of wider social forces, it is in its structures that all the antagonisms of class society come to a head, are concentrated. Politics is about the state, because the ultimate guarantee of a particular class's domination lies in its monopoly of force. Any study of politics which detaches the apparatuses of state power from their 'real foundations' in the forces and relations of production can offer only partial and one-sided insights, but any study which ignores these apparatuses simply misses the point.

6

One implication of this argument is that Marxism has a conflict theory of politics. Politics is the process through which classes with antagonistic interests struggle to obtain, retain or influence state power. Marxism is not alone in thus tracing the roots of politics to social conflict, but it differs from other such accounts in two important respects. First, it is commonplace to see politics as the mechanism

[17]   K. Marx, *Grundrisse* (Harmondsworth, 1973), p. 108.
[18]   N. Poulantzas, *State, Power, Socialism* (London, 1978), p. 129.

through which conflicts of interest are resolved, and social equilibrium thus secured. Such a view is to be found, for example, in the political writings of Talcott Parsons, and in Andrew Dunsire's contribution to this collection (see chapter 5). Marxism denies that politics can resolve the conflicts which generate it. On the contrary, as the product of class antagonism, it is, in words of Engels that I have already quoted, 'the admission that society has become entangled in an insoluble contradiction with itself', a contradiction which can be resolved only by the transformation of that society, that is, by social revolution.

Secondly, accounts of politics which locate its origins in social conflicts tend to treat such conflicts as permanent and ineradicable features of human life. Skilful political leadership, what Graeme Moodie calls the art of governing, may be able to manage, and even perhaps to overcome some particular conflict, but never to eliminate social conflict as such. Conflict, the struggle between rival groups, is endemic to human society, and thus will continue to generate politics however great the transformations undergone by economic and social arrangements.

Once again, such a view of social life (whose greatest exponents are perhaps Thomas Hobbes, Freidrich Nietzsche and Max Weber) runs counter to Marxism. For if politics is a product of class antagonism then it is a historically limited phenomenon – in two respects. Not only does politics have relatively recent origins, in the past few millennia of class-division and state-formation, but it cannot survive the elimination of class antagonisms.

Marx himself argued that his greatest originality lay in establishing that class society itself is a transient phenomenon. 'My own contribution was 1) to show that the *existence of classes* is merely bound up with certain historical *phases in the development of production,* 2) that the class struggle necessarily leads to the *dictatorship of the proletariat,* 3) that the dictatorship itself constitutes no more than the transition to the *abolition of all classes* and to a *classless society.*' [19]

Marx's lifework, *Capital,* is devoted to showing that capitalism is distinguished from other forms of class society in that it creates both the material and the social conditions of a classless, communist society. It does so materially by abolishing scarcity. The existence of classes depends ultimately on the low productivity of labour, which permits a

[19]   *CW*, XXXIX, pp. 62 and 65.

minority to live off the labour of the rest, but condemns the majority to a lifetime of drudgery. Capitalism, whose dynamic and revolutionary character Marx praises to the heavens in the *Communist Manifesto*, so develops the productive forces that the material basis of classes no longer exists. Today we find that even existing food production is sufficient to support the world's population at an adequate standard of living. The 'scarcity' thanks to which 800 million people in the third world go hungry is artificial, brought about by capitalist relations of production which make it unprofitable to feed the poor.

7

Capitalism also creates the social conditions for communism. It does so by creating the working class, 'a class constantly increasing in numbers, and trained, united and organized by the very mechanism of the capitalist process of production'.[20] Capitalism exploits workers collectively, bringing them together into large units of production where they are involved in increasingly socialized labour processes. Consequently, when workers resist their exploitation they do so collectively, creating organizations such as trade unions which depend for their power on the strength workers share within production. Marx believed that the class struggle between labour and capital would develop from a purely economic, trade-union conflict, into a political struggle, oriented on the state, and culminating in its overthrow, and the establishment of institutions of workers' power in which the majority would for the first time exercise direct political control. But even this new, and radically democratic form of state, which Marx called the dictatorship of the proletariat, would be a temporary phenomenon (the Roman dictators ruled only for six months). In the higher phase of communism, in which the further development of the productive forces would finally eradicate class antagonisms, the social basis for any form of specialized repressive apparatus would no longer exist. The state, in Engels' famous phrase, withers away.

Marxism is thus a theory of the abolition of politics. For it anticipates and seeks to achieve a communist society in which neither classes nor the state exist. Even more paradoxically, it pursues the abolition of politics

---

[20]   Marx, *Capital* I, p. 929.

by political means. For the precondition of the creation of a classless society is the conquest of political power by the working class. This apparent paradox is resolved by the fact that the state created by this revolution, the dictatorship of the proletariat, is, as Lenin put it, 'no longer a state in the proper sense of the word'.[21] Marx's model for such a state was the Paris Commune in which the 'special bodies of armed men', the army and police, were disbanded, and replaced by the armed people. The state in the sense of 'a public power which no longer directly coincides with the population organizing itself as an armed force' is destroyed, and replaced by democratically organized institutions of working-class power.

8

It would be the mildest of understatements to say that the Marxist view of politics is a controversial one, and indeed certainly not one widely shared by practitioners of the discipline of Politics. So scandalous, so implausible does this view seem that even many Marxists feel obliged to reject or at least to qualify its main propositions.

The most common reason given for disagreement with the Marxist theory of politics lies in its supposed assimilation of all forms of social conflict and inequality to class antagonism. This central objection lies behind many of the more familiar criticisms of Marxism, of which the following are some examples. What about non-state societies – surely they involve conflict? Has the state withered away in the 'really existing socialism' of the eastern bloc? Can racial and sexual inequalities be reduced to class exploitation? Is the modern liberal – democratic state (or indeed its absolutist predecessor) merely a coercive class institution? Obviously, it is impossible to respond adequately here to the accusation of 'class reductionism' that lies at the heart of all these objections. I shall restrict myself to two clarifications.

The first is that Marxism is not compelled to assert that no conflict would exist in a classless, stateless society. Trotsky argued that, under communism,

> there will be the struggle for one's opinion, for one's project, for one's taste. In the measure in which political struggles will be

---

[21] Lenin, *Collected Works*, XXV, p. 468.

> eliminated – and in a society where there are no classes, there will be
> no such struggles – the liberated passions will be channelized into
> techniques, into construction which also includes art . . . . People will
> divide into 'parties' over the question of a new gigantic canal, or the
> distribution of oases in the Sahara (such a question will exist too), over
> the regulation of the weather and the climate, over a new theatre, over
> chemical hypotheses, over two competing tendencies in music, and over
> a best system in sports.[22]

So the claim is not that there will be no conflict in a communist
society, but rather that such social struggles as do take place will not be
generated by antagonistic conflicts of interest arising from relations of
class exploitation, and so will not require a specialized apparatus of
repression to regulate their outcome. Indeed, some Marxists have gone
further and argued that, far from suppressing individuality, a
communist society would be the first actually to permit its full
expression. Such a society would be, in the words of the philosopher
Theodor Adorno, 'one in which people could be different without
fear'.[23]

The second point is this. While Marxism does not claim that *all*
conflict is a product of class antagonism, it does seek to explain the deep
and pervasive inequalities characteristic of modern society in terms of
their place in a system of class exploitation. This includes such
inequalities as racial and sexual oppression which on the face of it have
nothing to do with class. Many of the long-standing reproaches to
Marxism on this score have been given additional force by the
emergence in recent years of feminist and black nationalist movements
which strongly reject any such 'class reductionism'.

Yet it is precisely Marxism's insistence on accounting for social
inequalities and political struggles (including those between nation-
states) in terms of the master-concepts of the forces and relations of
production which make it such a bold and challenging scientific
hypothesis. It may indeed seem counter-intuitive to say that the
oppression of women owes its persistence today to the capitalist mode
of production. But it is characteristic of any serious scientific theory that
it runs counter to some common-sense intuitions.

A historical analogy may help to make Marxism's very strong claim

---

[22] L. Trotsky, *Literature and Revolution* (Ann Arbor, 1971), pp. 230–1.
[23] T. W. Adorno, *Minima Moralia* (London, 1974), p. 103.

seem less scandalous. In the seventeenth century a handful of thinkers developed what Bernard Williams has called an 'absolute conception of reality'.[24] They argued that many of the properties of a physical object which are most relevant to human beings' everyday experience – its potential uses, location, tactile and visual qualities, etc. – were at best secondary to understanding its behaviour. For the purpose of science, what counted was those properties which could be analysed by means of mathematical concepts. The authors of this profoundly unpalatable view, which expelled from the physical universe meaning, quality and purpose, were the founders of modern Physics. Three and a half centuries have borne witness to the correctness of their highly counter-intuitive beliefs.

This analogy does not in itself lend any credibility to the central claim of Marxism. But it reminds us that the test of this claim, as of any scientific hypothesis, lies in the degree of its success in explaining and anticipating events in the world. Marxism is an empirical theory, and must be judged as such. Once the issue is posed in these terms, then what is striking is how formidable a tradition of political analysis Marxism has developed. Marx's writings on France; Luxemburg's discussions of the Russian revolution of 1905 and the German revolution of 1918; the vast body of work in which Lenin undertook the 'concrete analysis of concrete situations'; Trotsky's analyses of the driving forces of the Russian revolution, of the causes of its subsequent degeneration, and of the rise of German fascism; and Gramsci's studies of the manner in which political power is held and overthrown – all these put in the shade anything that conventional political scientists or theorists have been able to come up with.

9

But, of course, traditions only live if they are continued. They have to be continually renewed and refashioned by work which, while building on the achievements of the past, seeks to go beyond them. For a generation, first the triumphs of Stalinism and fascism, and then the post-war stabilization of capitalism ensured that the classical Marxist tradition was confined to the margins of political and intellectual life. It

---

[24] B. A. O. Williams, *Descartes* (Harmondsworth, 1978).

is only in the past fifteen years, with the return of economic crises and social and political conflict to the west, that Marxism has enjoyed a revival. The challenge is to develop the Marxist approach to politics, one that is holist and historical, that is both concerned to study political institutions and processes in their historical specificity, and ready to relate them to the social whole and the contradictions which constitute it.

The matter cannot, however, rest here. The scandal of Marxism for the discipline of Politics does not lie in its theoretical claims. Marxism is not merely a scientific research programme, but a practical movement whose goal is socialist revolution as a preliminary to the creation of a classless society. Marxism challenges the separation of theory and practice characteristic of the bourgeois academy. 'The philosophers have only *interpreted* the world in various ways,' Marx wrote in the Eleventh Thesis on Feuerbach, 'the point is to *change* it.'[25] Marxism not only denies the discipline of Politics an epistemological foundation. It seeks to abolish politics itself by eradicating the class antagonisms which generate it. The greatest Marxist students of politics were also practitioners of politics – Marx and Engels, Lenin and Trotsky, Luxemburg and Gramsci. As long as politics exists, it cannot be ignored.

[25]   *CW*, V, p. 5.

8

A discipline of Politics?

DAVID HELD AND ADRIAN LEFTWICH

1

Politics denotes an activity about which many people today feel a combination of cynicism, scepticism and mistrust. It is experienced as something distant and remote from everyday life. The affairs of government and national politics are not things many people claim to understand, nor are they a source of sustained interest. Not surprisingly perhaps, those closest to both power and privilege are the ones who have most interest in and are most favourable to political life. For the rest, the fact that something is a recognizably 'political' statement is almost enough to bring it instantly into disrepute – it marks the statement as in all probability a strategic utterance and an evasion of the truth. Politics is, thus, a 'dirty' word, associated frequently with self-seeking behaviour, hypocrisy and 'public relations' activity geared to selling policy packages to those who might otherwise purchase elsewhere. Accordingly, people often mistrust and dislike politicians, who are thought to be concerned first and foremost with their own careers and hence all too likely to sidestep pressing questions and to downplay or ignore problems.[1]

The discipline of Politics does little, if anything, to dispel this image of politics and politicians. Focusing as it often does on the nature and structure of government as a decision-making process and on those who press their claims upon it, it portrays politics as a distinct and separate sphere in society, a sphere set apart from, for instance, personal, family

[1] The evidence for Britain is summarized in the Open University publication by David Held, 'Power and Legitimacy in Contemporary Britain', in *State and Society* (Milton Keynes, 1984).

and business life.[2] By focusing on governmental institutions, the
discipline of Politics marginalizes and provides little basis for
understanding the very stuff of politics, that is, those deep-rooted
problems that actually face us all daily as citizens, for example issues of
war and peace, unemployment and technical change, inequality and
conflict. It is one of the claims of this chapter that a discipline of Politics
which fails to address systematically these problems reinforces the
widely held notion of politics as a more or less unworthy activity for the
self-interested. It is our belief that the discipline of Politics does
qenerally fail to address central problems and to develop the necessary
originality and skills for their resolution. It is not therefore a surprise
that the initial commitment, enthusiasm and keenness which many
students bring to the study of politics is gradually but steadily eroded,
giving way to a preoccupation with learning (memorizing) a set
curriculum and with individual examination performance.

2

We live in a world which is increasingly punctuated by crises which
daily affect the welfare and life-chances of countless millions of human
beings. For instance, one can point to evidence of major and often
increasing inequalities within societies between, say, classes, cultures,
sexes and regions, in respect of the ownership or control of crucial
resources, or access to them, whether these be land, capital, income or
jobs. The rising tide of unemployment in most societies is one concrete
manifestation of this, with all the enormous personal and social costs
this brings about, and the waste of human resources it represents. Stark
contrasts are often associated with it. In the United Kingdom, for
instance, as unemployment climbs – especially in areas like Merseyside
and the North-east, and particularly amongst the young and the ethnic
minorities – it may seem paradoxical to find that the number of
private new cars sold in the first half of 1983 was greater than in the
same period in 1982. And, although at least eleven million people –
wage earners and their dependants – live on wages *below* the poverty
line, a new branch of the expensive Parisian restaurant, Maxime's, can

---

[2] As such, its premises are consistent with those of classical liberalism. See David Held, 'Central
Perspectives on the Modern State', in David Held et al. (eds), *States and Societies* (Oxford, 1983).

open in London (at £30 per head, minimum) in the midst of this.[3] In many parts of the third world – notably Asia and Latin America – the number of landless poor and urban unemployed increases each year, while small and extremely wealthy elites live in conditions of more or less sumptuous luxury, often in houses and estates guarded by dogs, high fences and electronic security devices.

One can point, too, at the increasing militarization of the globe in terms of escalating national expenditures on arms, the swelling number of military personnel, the booming trade in arms exports and the steady build-up of nuclear warheads. The evidence shows that, increasingly, civilians are the main casualties of war, that between 1960 and 1982 there have been some sixty-five major wars and that, at a conservative estimate, nearly eleven million lives have been lost in them.[4] Famines often erupt in the wake of such conflicts. But they also occur where there have been no such conflicts and where, as often as not, national and global food availability has been no worse and sometimes better than in previous non-famine years. They even occur where food is being exported from the country concerned.[5]

A glance at the annual reports of organizations like Amnesty International will show, in addition, a dismal global record on human rights, as more or less repressive regimes emerge to try to stamp out the opposition to such inequalities and the attempts by the dispossessed, deprived or powerless to alter them.

Moreover, it is simply not the case that these problems occur in isolation of each other in particular societies. As often as not they are related, sometimes directly and sometimes in long, looping chains of cause and effect. It is also clear that the people who are usually most directly affected by these events have little control over the forces which may cause them, since major decisions which influence their lives are often taken thousands of miles away. For example, a decision, or threatened decision, to suspend US food aid to Bangladesh, taken in the air-conditioned White House in Washington, may stimulate the sudden escalation of food prices in Dacca and contribute directly to the

---

[3] *Guardian*, 11 July 1983, and 1 November, 1983.
[4] Ruth Leger Sivard, *World Military and Social Expenditures, 1982* (Leesburg, Virginia, 1982).
[5] Amartya Sen, *Poverty and Famines* (Oxford, 1982); and F. M. Lappé and J. Collins, *Food First: The Myth of Scarcity* (London, 1980).

outbreak of famine amongst the urban and rural poor.[6] Or the board of directors of a transnational corporation, coolly assessing its global operations from their headquarters in New York, London, Paris or Tokyo, may decide to shift production of one of its lines from one country to another, thus creating unemployment in a town at a stroke. Or the decision by a government in west or east to suspend or step up military aid to one side or another in a political struggle in a distant country may decisively influence the outcome of that conflict, or fan it into a further vortex of violence. Or the International Monetary Fund (IMF), pursuing a particular line of economic policy, may insist as a condition of its loan to a government that the latter cut public expenditure, devalue its currency and pull back on subsidized welfare programmes. This may provoke hunger and anger amongst the urban poor, bring about bread riots and perhaps the fall of a government, or it might contribute directly to the imposition of martial law.[7] In each and every one of these and many other instances, the effect on human lives and conditions is inevitably far-reaching and sometimes devastating.

3

Now it is central to the argument of this chapter that politics, as we shall shortly define the activity, is at the heart of all such problems. Any discipline advertising itself as Politics must therefore engage with such issues, and it must seek to train those who study it to analyse, understand and hence know how, potentially, to act upon them, though there may certainly be more than one course of action which flows from such understanding. It is our contention that the discipline of Politics as conventionally taught has in general failed to do this. We shall explain, first, why we think this has happened and we shall go on, second, to suggest what can and should be done to try to remedy the situation.

We recognize that it is both a difficult and delicate time to raise some of these questions, for the social sciences in general, and Politics in particular, do not currently enjoy rave notices nor wholehearted

[6] Donald F. McHenry and Kai Bird, 'Food Bungle in Bangladesh', *Foreign Policy* 27 (Summer, 1977); and Rehman Sobhan, 'Politics of Food and Famine in Bangladesh', *Economic and Political Weekly*, 1 December 1979.

[7] Instances of this have occurred in recent years in various third-world societies − for example, Jamaica, Egypt and Sudan. For a useful account of the IMF and the third world see Norman Girvan, 'Swallowing the IMF Medicine in the Seventies', *Development Dialogue* 2 (1980).

support from the state or private funding agencies. Indeed the social sciences (with Sociology as the main target) are often thought of as irrelevant or subversive. They are said not to engage with the 'real problems' of society, but to involve themselves in highly abstract and largely internecine theoretical debates on abstruse questions of analytic method or substance. There is some truth in this view, as any teacher or student in a social science department will readily acknowledge. But there is something fundamentally specious in the criticism about 'irrelevance' when it comes from those – usually in the media or the official agencies of government responsible for higher education – who *do not want* social scientists to engage in 'relevant' work, except at the 'technical' margins, lest they be critical of the fundamental principles of policy and practice of state and society, whether in the west or east, north or south. When social scientists do engage with controversial matters they are more than likely to find their research funds, jobs and – in certain parts of the globe – their citizenship or even their lives under direct attack. [8]

Moreover, it is unnecessary for social scientists always to apologize for theoretical interests: scientific work does progress, and can only progress, through work of this kind. But underlying the argument of this chapter is the claim that the kinds of problems indicated above are not only real and urgent, they are relevant and profoundly *political.* If the discipline of Politics is to live up to its name, then it must engage directly and theoretically with such problems, by confronting the analytical and pedagogic issues necessary for their understanding and potential resolution, in theory and in practice.

The difficulty, of course, is that problems of this kind are inherently interdisciplinary, involving complex *relations* between aspects of social life which are conventionally thought of and studied (wrongly in our view) as distinct: such as economy, polity, social structure and international relations. It is the interplay of *all* these phenomena which we regard as politics: what we would call the lived interdisciplinarity of all collective social life. Hence if Politics as a discipline is to be taken seriously it must, paradoxically, be interdisciplinary, so that it can develop the explanatory frameworks and teaching methods which enable its students to come to grips with such problems and their

---

[8] For example, research funds and jobs have been lost in Britain; the citizenship of some social scientists has been effectively withdrawn in some east European societies; and social scientists have been murdered in Chile, Argentina and South Africa in recent years.

possible solutions. It cannot treat politics as a separate institutional sphere, as only the officially 'public' realm of government.

Before proceeding to examine some of these questions, we offer, first, a broad working definition of politics.

In our view, politics is a phenomenon found in and between all groups, institutions (formal and informal) and societies, cutting across public and private life. It is involved in all the relations, institutions and structures which are implicated in the activities of production and reproduction in the life of societies. It is expressed in all the activities of co-operation, negotiation and struggle over the use, production and distribution of resources which this entails. Politics creates and conditions all aspects of our lives, and is at the core of the development of problems in society and the collective modes of their resolution. Thus politics is about power; about the forces which influence and reflect its distribution and use; and about the effect of this on resource use and distribution; it is about the 'transformative capacity' of social agents, agencies and institutions: it is not about Government or government alone.[9] Where politics is regarded more narrowly as a sphere apart from economy or culture, that is as governmental activity and institutions, a vast domain of what we would consider politics is excluded from view. There is, in fact, nothing *more political* than the constant attempts to exclude certain types of issues from politics. These attempts represent strategies of depoliticization; that is, strategies to have certain issues treated as if they were not a proper subject for politics. Classic examples of this are the constant attempts to make the organization of the economy in the west, or violence against women in marriage (assault or rape), thought of as non-political – a mere outcome of 'free' private contracts.[10] Furthermore, administrators and politicians often ask us to 'keep politics out' of things like sport (or vice versa), or not to 'mix' politics with religion or industrial relations or 'race' relations. What they are *actually* asking is that we *refrain* from participating in politics, that is in decisions about the use and distribution of resources in relation to affairs that are very important to our lives. As such, they are not seeking to promote, defend or even

---

[9] For a discussion of power as 'transformative capacity' see Anthony Giddens, *Central Problems in Social Theory* (London, 1979).

[10] An excellent discussion connecting issues about marriage to politics and Politics can be found in Carole Pateman, 'Feminism and Democracy', in Graeme Duncan (ed.), *Democratic Theory and Practice* (Cambridge, 1983).

isolate politics, they are seeking to *suppress* it.[11] To study politics, therefore, is to study critically the history of possibilities and the possibilities of history.

4

We stated in the previous section that the discipline of Politics as conventionally taught fails to engage with the central problems of politics in both modern and historical societies. Why is this the case? In addressing this question we make a number of points. Some have to do with higher education more broadly, some with the social and historical sciences generally, and some with Politics in particular.

(1) The first critical matter is the remarkable degree of specialization that has occurred between disciplines (and within them), especially since the second world war. The division of labour in the humanities and social sciences is highly advanced and the resulting 'output' highly fragmented. While specialization need not always lead to fragmentation, this has in fact happened within both the natural and social sciences and – most dramatically – in the sharp divisions between them. Specialist research proliferates in every field, and it gets more specialized. The almost tidal flow of learned articles, journals and books is overwhelming. New kinds of information-processing systems (such as bibliographies of bibliographies) have emerged in an effort to help students and academic staff to keep up with what has been written. Other than full-time researchers (and seldom amongst them), most of us find it increasingly difficult to keep up, even within our often tight specialisms.

The general problem with specialization in science is that while it may yield highly detailed research and understanding of *particular* parts of problems, it is almost always the case that these accounts are partial and one-sided ones. And while there have been important advances made in the specialist study of *parts* of the social world and its problems, this has not been matched by comparable advances in attempts to integrate these into wider frameworks of understanding about our societies and their politics. To put it bluntly, we seem to know more about the parts and less about the whole; and the trouble is that we risk

[11]   Adrian Leftwich, *Redefining Politics: People, Resources and Power* (London, 1983), p. 26.

knowing very little even about the parts because their context and conditions of existence in the whole are eclipsed from view. Moreover, in the course of this specialization and fragmentation, as different disciplines (and special interests within them) have fastened on to *bits* of problems for analytical attention, the explanation of relations *between* the bits has become the concern of none. Specific disciplines, that is to say, have identified their corners of the problem, and departed with them. This is the consequence of specialization. But the complex character of the whole problem has remained unexplained (and certainly unresolved) because – as we pointed out earlier – such problems are simply not amenable to narrow disciplinary analysis or technical treatment.

Within the social sciences it is clear that, broadly speaking, 'the economy', 'the social system' and 'the political system' (though not always called that) have been thought of and studied as if they were more or less autonomous spheres of activity in human societies. This is reflected in the conventionally rigorous separation of the disciplines of Economics, Sociology and Politics (or Political Science or Government), and their main concerns. Within each, soaring levels of sometimes breathtakingly abstract theories have emerged, and the more abstract the levels, the further the disciplines have moved away from the complex relations of problems in societies, in all their murky and involved real-world character; and the further they have diverged from each other.

In the natural sciences, the closer one approaches the explanation of a *particular* phenomenon or problem – the structure or malfunctioning of the human body; or pollution; or the weather; or an epizootic – the less and less possible it is to maintain sharp distinctions between disciplines. The same is true for more obviously social and political problems – inflation, unemployment, inequality, poverty and famines, conflict in the third world, and so on. Yet their study tends to be confined to particular disciplinary corners with persistently disappointing results, such as the failure to produce an adequate theory of inflation and unemployment.

In Politics the focus on narrow institutional spheres of government and associated political matters, as conventionally understood, has led to wholly inadequate accounts, for instance, of the sources and forms of power in societies. Much standard democratic theory as taught at undergraduate level, for example, has not turned its attention to the enormous concentrations of power in the private and corporate sector of 'the economy', because they are usually considered to be beyond the borders of 'the political system' or simply not political. The daily and lived interdependence of 'polity' and 'economy', of state and society, and of nations with one another have not been at the centre of the discipline's pedagogic concerns.

(2) It is not too difficult to see why this state of affairs has come about and how it has been reproduced in the politics of Politics. As Graeme Moodie indicated in chapter 1, the twin pillars of studies in Politics in Britain have been political institutions and political theory. The latter provides the clue to the main lineages of the discipline, in Constitutional History, Law and Philosophy. In the post-war years this has been influenced by the behavioural approaches of American Political Science, and by a variety of streams of Marxism. Nonetheless, it remains fair to say that the pillars stand more or less intact, if somewhat weather-beaten, though around them have grown up more or less strong but minor areas such as political sociology, international relations (some-times in separate departments) and third-world studies. There has also been a proliferation of diverse special interests, including political anthropology, public administration and electoral studies.

Hence traditionalism (the twin pillars) and a multiplicity of specialisms have characterized the academic discipline of Politics. With more or less consistency, succeeding generations of graduate students have been socialized into these main streams and have hence sustained the continuity of approach, with interesting but not decisive shifts in orientation of the discipline as a whole.

It is important to recognize that in its theoretical and institutional concerns, the discipline of Politics has continued to be subject-centred, not problem-oriented, in respect of both content and methods of teaching. By this we mean that it proceeds on the assumption that there is a body of knowledge to communicate to students – for instance, what Locke, Hobbes, Mill and Marx said; or the distinction between congressional and parliamentary modes of government. In general the discipline has not been concerned to develop and deploy particular kinds of analytical skills for the purposes of engaging with, and trying to resolve (at least at the level of explanation) the kinds of problems which continue to occur in and between societies and which – as argued earlier – are the core of politics.

(3) Institutions of higher education have many objectives and a

variety of functions; these include research, teaching, the transmission of a culture and other services to the community. Whatever may be the proper balance between these, it is generally the case that, as far as teaching is concerned, a claim is made to provide a training which promotes such capacities as, *inter alia*, 'the general powers of the mind', 'critical ability', 'thinking for oneself', 'insight', 'self-education', 'judgement' and so forth. All major reports and books on the question over the last two decades have rightly emphasized the importance of these capacities (although the particular conceptions of them are by no means always ones with which we would agree). [12] Do institutions of higher education actually promote these capacities?

We all know that the vast majoirity of undergraduates do not go on to *use* what they have 'learned' in their courses (and this is as true for Biology and Chemistry as it is for the social sciences). We also know from memory-retention studies that, if not used, such 'knowledge' disappears down the memory curve within not too many months. So it is important that the different disciplines (subjects, that is) should be more the media through which general capacities and skills are developed, and less the substance of 'learning'. Yet, in practice, teaching of 'subjects' rather than skills is the norm. In the social and historical sciences, especially, the lecture, the seminar, the tutorial, the essay or dissertation and the unseen examination still prevail as the main modes of teaching, learning and assessment. These methods, linked to the content of the 'subject' (in the books), have the effect of inducing a kind of passive *consumption* of knowledge, rather than stimulating active participation and the *production* of analyses, explanations and resolutions of problems through the development of skills. Passivity and consumer orientations are reinforced by the sheer volume of books and articles students have to digest – a quantity of material which no superperson could ever cope with in the time allotted and which leaves most ordinary mortals frequently bewildered. Anyone who has written essays and exams knows that these exercises are by and large concerned with the re-presentation of standard material in the field; they know additionally what is expected from them in particular cases and will adjust their presentations accordingly. On the other side, anyone who is involved in marking essays, dissertations and examination papers will concede, quite readily in fact, that the overwhelming bulk of them do

[12]   See, for instance the *Report of the Committee on University Teaching* (the Hale Report) (London, 1964); and the *Report of the Committee on Higher Education* (the Robbins Report) (London, 1963).

not show 'independent thought' or 'critical ability'. Those involved in marking regularly find a superficiality of thought, the recycling of certain sets of standard ideas or fashionable orthodoxies of one kind or another, a lack of originality, a fragmentation of understanding through disciplinary monism, and – above all – an incapacity to cope analytically with the *de facto* interdisciplinarity of a difficult world and its complex problems.

A common response to all this from weary and perhaps cynical academics is to blame the 'poor quality' of students these days, the depressed and groggy state of mind in which some students come to higher education after the grim grind of A-level swotting (or the equivalent final high-school examinations in the USA and Europe), or more generally the 'lack of student interest'. But how often, in Politics particularly, do we look to ourselves as the bearers of the discipline, to our pedagogy and the institutional arrangements (for instance departmental and course structures) as possible sources of the academic malaise we may diagnose?

It can certainly be said that many students come up to higher education as enthusiasts. The political problems of the world are a source of major interest to them. And then, to put it crudely, we anaesthetize their interests and enthusiasms by dragging them more or less unwillingly through 'the subject', and by feeding them or telling them to find out and learn a body of theoretical ideas and empirical information which (with notable exceptions) – in Economics as well as Politics and Sociology – seldom seems to engage with the 'relevant' issues and *problems* of one's own society (or those abroad).

(4) It is important to qualify some of the arguments above. There *are* areas where interdisciplinary work seeks to establish links between the concerns and insights of different disciplines. There *are* areas where courses start with problems. In the developing work in Ecology, for instance, important links are being made and taught in the analysis of problems that flow from the relations between human communities and their actions upon the environment, and vice versa. [13] And in the work done in political sociology, development studies and the approach of political economists, there are important contributions being made.

But in general it remains true to say that, as a discipline, Politics has remained largely bound to its lineage. It has encouraged the more or less

[13] Rowland Moss, *The Ecology of Human Communities,* an Inaugural Address (Birmingham, 1974).

idiosyncratic research of graduate students and staff within its traditional institutional and theoretical concerns; it has continued to stress the teaching of traditional philosophical and empirical bodies of information in standard ways; it has not expanded its concerns to engage with relevant *problems* in historical and contemporary societies; and it has been more or less haphazard about identifying and training the analytical skills and capacities which are needed for tackling such problems.

What, then, can or should be done?

5

It is not possible in a short piece such as this to spell out in every detail the central components of a discipline of Politics with respect to syllabus and method, at least as far as undergraduate courses and research priorities are concerned. Nor is it desirable, for there is enormous scope for variety in terms of structure, approach and use of distinctive kinds of illustrative theoretical and empirical materials. But what we can do is to outline the central principles and preoccupations which, in our view, should form the organizing framework and pedagogic priorities of a discipline of Politics.[14] It should be clear from what follows that these flow from the definition of politics given above; they are concerned with providing the historical, comparative and analytical understandings and skills which will enable students to handle the problems of our societies and their futures more adequately.

Starting first with the kinds of skills and understandings which students of Politics should acquire, we would stress four main (and to a significant degree overlapping) areas. First, there are conceptual/analytical skills. By this we mean the ability to analyse, use, defend and criticize concepts and terms found in political debate, historical and modern (concepts like 'sovereignty', 'freedom', 'justice', 'equality', 'democracy' and 'coercion'). This involves appreciation of the historical origins, meanings and usages of such concepts, and the development of

---

[14]   What follows draws heavily on a set of proposals for an Honours degree in Politics which were formulated by a group of six in the Politics department in the University of York in the course of the discussions referred to in the Introduction to this volume. We acknowledge here the contribution to those proposals by our friends and colleagues Alex Callinicos, Bill Fuller, David Skidmore and Albert Weale.

the capacity to engage in political argument about them. Clarity of understanding is a necessary condition of effective political analysis. But it is not a sufficient condition. For it is essential, if one is to appreciate how political life generally is and can be shaped by ideas, to learn the way in which concepts actually function in particular political arguments and contexts. We do not, therefore, see the *theorists* of these concepts and practices as being the starting point for achieving such an understanding. Rather, we would stress the use of concrete *problems* and *debates* as the starting point, and as the means of approaching the theorists (whether they be Mill, Weber or Marx). As an initial illustration one could take a much publicized debate on many British campuses some ten years ago as to whether certain speakers should be allowed to visit the colleges and give lectures. Using that issue of 'free speech' and the arguments which were developed for and against it at the time, students could be introduced with extraordinary intensity to wider theoretical concerns about 'freedom' and the rights and obligations of citizens.[15] Through such instances, not only does the pertinence of difficult questions become apparent, but the implications and consequences of various judgements as well. Many other issues could be used in similar ways. For instance, in both the west and east (and also in the south) many societies advertise their political arrangements as 'democratic'. Are these arrangements the same? If not, how do they differ? And why? How do the distinctive meanings and practices relate to classical and modern theories of democracy? Do the theories help us to grasp and justify particular arrangements? If so, which ones? Can the arrangements be developed and improved? If so, how, and according to what principles and under what conditions? The same kind of approach can be adopted with other central concepts of political discourse. When ministers of state and policy-makers of one kind or another refer, for instance, in the west or east, to the defence of 'freedom', what do they mean? Do the !Kung San of the Kalahari have a notion of 'freedom' which is different to that of transnational corporations in their wish to defend their 'freedom' from state 'interference'? Can we diagnose the distinctive meanings used, and the social and historical contexts of their evolution? In what ways can the various conceptions of 'freedom' in political theory illuminate the problem? Can they help us disentangle rhetoric and self-interest from

[15] This has been done with much success in the Politics department in the University of York in an introductory course on political theory, devised largely by David Edwards.

clarity, consistency and sound judgement? Through the pursuit of such an approach one becomes better equipped not only to recognize good and bad arguments and the nature of different types of reasoning, but also to be clearer about what we can reasonably say about issues that concern us.

Secondly, there are theoretical/analytical skills. By this we mean the ability to understand, compare, criticize, defend and, above all, *use* rival theories about the nature and relations of politics, economics and social structure in the analysis of historical and modern societies. In building on and connecting with the previous set of conceptual skills (and of course they overlap) it is necessary again to stress the importance we attach to starting with problems, not bodies of theory. The problems should be used as a means of leading students to explore different kinds of theory with a view to assessing their value for explanatory purposes. Take unemployment as an example: given a set of facts and figures (themselves subject to methodological and logistical problems of definition and collection – an issue to be considered shortly), how can it be explained? Is it a problem found in all societies, past and present, or would one simply never have encountered it in traditional Maasai, Eskimo or ancient Greek society? If not, why not? When does it first emerge as a problem in human societies? With what set of conditions is it associated? If, as some theorists argue, it is intrinsic to free enterprise and capitalist societies, why then is it found also in so-called communist societies, in eastern Europe and China? The same approach can be adopted with respect to other problems of the kind mentioned at the start of this chapter: the patterns of escalating violence and conflict in the third world, or famines, or inequalities between nations, classes, regions and the sexes. First identify the problem and its dimensions in any particular instance. Then go on to examine what explanatory value there is in different general theories about the phenomenon (or aspects of it). This can be done at different levels of intensity and spread. Tutors and students may want to focus on a number of problems; or on one. It is quite possible by focusing on one problem to encompass progressively an enormous variety of theoretical questions. But however this is done, in one or more courses, we would stress the primacy of problem-related analysis, not theory-learning *per se*.

Thirdly, as should be clear from the above, there are essential skills required in the methods and modes of political enquiry and analysis. Few of the above objectives could be met if students were not able to develop a number of skills to do with thinking, counting and researching in politics; of how to gather, use and interpret information; of ways of putting arguments to various tests, or of how to assess both quantitative and qualitative judgements. A course – or a set of courses – concerned with developing such skills would be closely related to the previous two, and the next one, to be discussed shortly. We would want to argue for the centrality of such a course (or set of courses) running throughout an undergraduate degree, involving periods of intensive project work each year; perhaps learning statistical techniques, use of a computer, methods of obtaining data from library sources and information systems, or analysing and interpreting data so obtained or collected in the course of practical work. Of course, the kind of work done would depend on other aspects of the degree and would need to be closely related to them, with a careful eye to local issues, problems, resources and sources. But, once again, the starting point can most effectively be problems or issues. For instance, someone claims that the USA is more 'free' than the Soviet Union; or that Blacks in South Africa are 'better off' than anywhere else in Africa: what can be meant by such claims? Are there criteria which might be elaborated and evidence sought to enable comparisons to be made? Or what do official government statistics offer on a particular topic, for example poverty? How are such statistics generated? What concepts underpin them and how are the data interpreted? Project work, often best undertaken by groups and assessed as a collective endeavour, is an invaluable way of introducing problems and skills, and of enabling those who undertake them to participate actively in shaping their own learning. The scope for projects is simply enormous. At one end of the spectrum students might be interested to undertake a detailed analysis of the politics of their own department, university or students' union. Such an analysis might focus, for example, on the way sexual divisions in society are reflected and reproduced in the organization, teaching and research of a department.[16] Or they might be encouraged to explore in some detail the concept of 'class'. Can the concept be made more rigorous so as to be used more effectively in political argument and analysis? What implications do rival definitions have, and what evidence can be collected, and how, for illustrating arguments about class and class action? How, in turn, does this evidence square with

[16] Some of these issues are explored in Janet Siltanen and Michelle Stanworth (eds), *Women and the Public Sphere* (London, 1984).

wider theories about class in societies? Or at the other end of the spectrum – in the more hard-nosed sense of 'method' – students may be able to undertake polls on various attitudes and preferences about certain local, national or international issues. Such polls may be more or less complex, with an eye to correlations of attitudes as between classes, sexes, age-groups and occupations, etc.

Finally, before looking at some of the requirements and implications of this, it is necessary to stress the importance of comparative and historical skills and knowledge. The real laboratory for the social sciences is the history and structure of the enormous range of politics of past and present societies and the relations between them in time and space. It is essential that students of Politics have more than a passing familiarity with the ways in which historical and modern societies have organized, explained and justified their affairs – in productive, distributive, decision-making, social, cultural and ideological terms. For these represent the contexts within which the kinds of problems discussed earlier have arisen and do arise. There are a variety of ways in which such historical and comparative understanding can be achieved. But, in broad outline, it would at least seem essential to include elements of the following, with examples depending on other areas of the degree: politics in non-state societies; the emergence of states; the emergence of the modern state (Europe) and the development of world systems; comparative government and institutions of modern states; comparative politics in modern states, e.g. with respect to issues of class, race, sex, etc. Again, it is important to emphasize the need to integrate this component of a degree with the other skills discussed before. That is to say, while there may be virtue in historical knowledge for its own sake, a much more important case for such understanding in Politics is that it provides the *medium* through which the other skills can be developed and deployed, and the *context* within which the genesis of various theories, concepts and analyses can be appreciated and hence their implications for other contexts assessed.

6

It should be clear from the above that, in terms of emphasis, we see the development of a set of related analytical skills – and *not* simply the learning of certain bodies of theory and empirical (institutional) information – as being the core of a discipline of Politics. The skills, of course, will require understanding of conceptual, theoretical and philosophical approaches from a variety of traditions. The development of such skills will also require historical understanding and knowledge of institutional detail. Such skills can of course be developed in a great variety of different courses, whose structure, relations, sequence, intensity and spread will differ from department to department, as they should. But given the conception of politics we use here, it makes a lot of sense, in our view, for departments of Politics to look beyond their institutional boundaries to the availability of staff in other departments, within and beyond the social sciences. This is not simply an argument for more interdepartmental work or the proliferation of joint degrees; for it is often the case now that joint degrees are experienced by students as the least satisfactory, because the intimacy of intellectual concerns and relations between departments is usually minimal, their parts seldom cohere substantively, and the workload is excessive. The kind, content and shape of interdepartmental collaboration we envisage (though we have no illusions as to how difficult in practice it would be to organize and sustain under present circumstances) would not flow from some abstract commitment to interdisciplinarity, but from the specific requirements of the concrete problems being used for pedagogic purposes. If one thinks of some of the substantive problems we have mentioned above, it is apparent how valuable the contributions of, for instance, economists, economic and social historians, geographers, sociologists, ecologists and biologists would be to their understanding and resolution. And students of Politics need, crucially, to be able to know how to *use* and integrate these diverse specialisms and skills in the analysis of the problems before them.

Whatever the local scope and possibilities, we would also stress the importance of *coherence* in a Politics degree or course. At present most students treat the variety of courses they follow as almost entirely discrete and autonomous. They rarely make any serious connections between them. They treat their degrees as being made up of (no doubt) interesting but largely unrelated components. That is our fault, not theirs. But a discipline of Politics – whatever its scope and scale – which sought consciously to integrate its components through problem-related study would change this dramatically. And it would have very beneficial effects on the relations between tutors who sometimes go for years without contacts in other departments.

If students are to develop the kinds of skills we have been stressing, it is necessary to have a very serious look at the full range of possibilities of teaching and learning methods.[17] There is a case for some of the traditional methods of lecture, seminar, tutorial and essay, but they must be used and integrated intelligently in meeting wider pedagogic purposes. Given that we emphasize problem-analysis, the case for projects of many kinds is overwhelming. We do not mean projects only in the conventional sense of dissertations and individual research essays. There is a variety of possibilities, each of which will enable students and staff to explore topics in depth, either on their own or in groups. For instance, to avoid the usual pattern of individual student isolation (or intellectual agoraphobia), certain courses (or parts of courses) may be best organized through and around reading groups and collectively arranged endeavours. Again, it will depend on the problem for which the reading may be thought appropriate, and this in turn will depend on the clarity with which the *objectives* of the course (or the treatment of the problem) are defined.

Reading groups are often useful for the treatment of problems (or parts of problems) which require more or less detailed comparative textual analysis, and often for the examination of 'normative' questions. For instance, students may be required, as part of their course, to assess the arguments for and against a Bill of Rights and to devise one for a particular society and its constitution. A reading group which focused on some of the different accounts that have been offered of the appropriate set of rights, duties and obligations of citizens *vis-à-vis* the state (such as those of Socrates or Mill or Nozick, for instance) would be a useful part of such work. Such concerns could be broadened and made more complex in the cumulative build-up of a degree by, say, raising the question as to whether the 'right to work' or the 'right of adults of both sexes to be active parents' ought to be included in the Bill of Rights. If so, what implications follow for the organization of productive (that is, 'economic') life, child-care arrangements and the place of the state in them? And so on.

But group work involves much more than simply reading groups. In a department with particular interests and specialist skills in, for

---

[17] For further elaboration on some of these points, see Adrian Leftwich, 'The Politics of Case Study: Problems of Innovation in University Education', *Higher Education Review* 13(2) (1981); and also his 'Social Science, Social Relevance and the Politics of Educational Development', *International Journal of Educational Development* 1(3) (1982); Lewis Elton, 'Can Universities Change?', *Studies in Higher Education* 6(1) (1981).

instance, analysing and resolving problems of democratic participation (in organizations, communities or government – local and national), there would be enormous advantage in having groups of students actually go out into the community to look at the structure, processes and problems of local government, industrial organization and community participation, with a view to producing individual or collective projects. In so doing, they will be able to develop some of the research and enquiry skills (collection of information, interviewing, participant observation, assessment of data and so on) so necessary for political analysis and for the development of the kind of political imagination necessary to resolve problems.

What this type of work requires, from teaching staff, is the commitment of time and imaginative energy to help specify the problems and to ensure that sources and resources are available for students to tap. The problem may be of the more conventional kind (why has revolutionary change not occurred in the most advanced capitalist societies, as some versions of Marxist theory imply it should have?); or the problem may be one less usually tackled in Politics departments. For instance, has the collectivization of agricultural production been an effective means of overcoming the food problems of developing societies? What do the experiences of, say, Russia, China, Israel and Tanzania tell us about the forms, details and contexts of successful and unsuccessful collectivization?

In our experience, group work by students, focusing on a concrete problem, is one of the most effective means of liberating their energies and of realizing unfulfilled potential. It enables them to learn, through project and other work, about the intense complexity of politics and the causes, conditions and consequences of problems, past or present. In confronting problems of the kind offered here as examples one cannot avoid getting to grips with issues of an institutional, historical, theoretical and comparative kind. Students (and staff!) learn: how to track down and use relevant sources and resources (staff, library, field-work where appropriate); how to collect, interpret and argue about evidence; how to assess competing concepts and theories, especially with regard to their explanatory or practical usefulness; and how to organize their time and energy (in groups or singly) with project-writing deadlines in mind. It seems to us that lectures, essays, tutorials and formal seminars should *serve* and *complement* these kinds of active

and participatory learning methods, rather than being merely sub-
stitutes for them as they currently tend to be.

7

Given the conception of politics which we have outlined, and given the
political nature of the problems which face modern societies, it should
be clear why we argue for a radical rethink and restructuring of the
discipline of Politics. At the heart of the approach we suggest are three
major points: first, the discipline should shift its primary focus away
from its long preoccupation with the teaching of subjects (like theory
and institutions) to a more self-conscious concern with the analysis of
problems. For politics is, just as Politics should be, fundamentally
concerned with understanding and acting upon problems, with the
modes of their analysis and collective resolution. Secondly, it follows
that the appropriate pedagogic priorities of the discipline should be
the training and learning of appropriate analytical skills, not the
'learning' of bodies of theoretical and empirical information. This is not
to say that understanding of theory and evidence is unimportant: on the
contrary, it is vital. But what it does mean, thirdly, is that a discipline
of Politics should be concerned to train its students to be able to *use*
theory and evidence for the purposes of analysis and practical action.
    Politics (in both senses) is the discourse and struggle over the
organization of human possibilites: it is academic and practical. It is
concerned with both theoretical and practical questions, with far-
reaching organizational and institutional issues. This unity of the
theoretical and practical distinguishes it as a discipline from, say,
political philosophy, as it is most often taught. The latter considers and
espouses political principles, arguments and even arrangements,
independently of considering the conditions of their enactment or
realization. In so doing, it encourages at a certain level the arbitrary
choice of principles, and seemingly endless abstract debates about them.
Anthropology and Sociology, on the other hand, have generally tended
to focus on certain kinds of societies or on certain limited spheres of
social behaviour and relations within them. And much Economics, in
developing sophisticated ways of measuring the costs and benefits of

different courses of action, provides no real account of *why* some are chosen and some are not.

The political nature of the problems of the world in practice involve questions of *all* these kinds: the conflicts of interest between diverse social groups in the constitution and reproduction of distinctive societies; the clash of competing principles and philosophical preferences; the consideration of the costs and benefits to different social groups of different courses of action; and the conditions for, or constraints on, the realization of policies, programmes and options. It is precisely for this reason that there is no contradiction (except in semantic terms) to say that the discipline of Politics must be interdisciplinary in its focus and its frameworks.

In our view it is this complexity which makes politics so intriguing to students and also of the greatest importance in practice. At a time when the social sciences are under some threat, when contraction seems likely and when it is tempting to play safe, it is necessary to assert this importance again and again. The problems of the modern world will never be solved by technical innovations alone, but only by the development and transformation of our politics in ways that can more effectively shape the kind, and better organize the distribution, of such innovations. Only by defining its purposes in terms of the urgency of the times, and hence its research and teaching priorities in terms of the *kind* of approach suggested here, will the discipline of Politics be able to make a serious contribution to the definition and furtherance of human welfare, and to the eradication of the tarnished image of politics.

Further reading

Chapter 1: Politics is about government

Hannah Arendt, 'On Violence', in her *Crises of the Republic* (Harmondsworth, 1973).

Robert A. Dahl, *Modern Political Analysis* (Englewood Cliffs, New Jersey, 1963; 1976).

Maurice Duverger, *The Idea of Politics: The Uses of Power in Society* (London, 1966).

S. E. Finer, *Comparative Government* (Harmondsworth, 1974).

Charles E. Lindblom, *The Policy-Making Process* (Englewood Cliffs, New Jersey, 1970).

J. D. B. Miller, *The Nature of Politics* (Harmondsworth, 1962).

H. F. Pitkin, *The Concept of Representation* (Berkeley, California, 1967 and 1972).

F. F. Ridley (ed.), *Studies in Politics* (Oxford, 1975).

Simon Roberts, *Order and Dispute: An Introduction to Legal Anthropology* (Harmondsworth, 1979).

D. H. Wrong, *Power: Its Forms, Bases and Uses* (Oxford, 1979).

Chapter 2: Politics and force

H. Barclay, *People Without Government* (London, 1982).

B. Crick, *In Defence of Politics* (London, 1962; third edn, 1982).

R. A. Dahl, *Modern Political Analysis* (Englewood Cliffs, New Jersey, 1976).

David Easton, *The Political System: An Inquiry into the State of Political Science* (New York, 1953; second edn, 1971).

S. E. Finer, *Comparative Government* (Harmondsworth, 1974).

F. M. Frohock, 'The Structure of "Politics" ', *American Political Science*

Review LXXII (1978), pp. 859 – 70.

F. I. Greenstein and N. W. Polsby (eds), *Handbook of Political Science* (Reading, Mass., 1975), vol. I.

J. D. B. Miller, *The Nature of Politics* (London, 1962).

P. P. Nicholson, 'What is Politics: Determining the Scope of Political Science', *Il Politico* XLII (1977), pp. 228 – 48.

D. D. Raphael, *Problems of Political Philosophy* (London, 1970; revised edn, 1976).

G. H. Sabine, *A History of Political Theory* (New York, 1937; fourth edn, revised by T. L. Thorson, Hinsdale, Illinois, 1973).

Carl Schmitt, *The Concept of the Political,* translation, Introduction and Notes by G. Schwab (New Brunswick, 1976).

A. Southall, 'Stateless Society', *International Encyclopaedia of the Social Sciences* XV, pp. 157 – 68.

Chapter 3: Politics as collective choice

A good introduction to British and American politics using collective choice theory is Iain McLean, *Dealing in Votes* (Oxford, 1982). A good general introduction is Michael Laver, *The Politics of Private Desires* (Harmondsworth, 1981). The paradox of voting is treated with some sophistication in Duncan Black, *The Theory of Committees and Elections* (Cambridge, 1958). The 'free rider' problem was first elaborated by Mancur Olson, *The Logic of Collective Action* (Cambridge, Mass., 1965), a classic work. The best recent summary of much relevant literature, some of it quite technical, is provided by William H. Riker, *Liberalism Against Populism* (San Francisco, 1982). Two original books that range widely are: Anatol Rapoport, *Fights, Games and Debates* (Ann Arbor, 1960), and Thomas C. Schelling, *Micromotives and Macrobehaviour* (New York and London, 1978). And, for those who like elegant mathematics with their social science, the following two books provide excellent examples: R. D. Luce and H. Raiffa, *Games and Decisions* (New York, 1957), and Michael Taylor, *Anarchy and Cooperation* (New York and London, 1976).

Chapter 4: Politics: people, resources and power

Given the particular definition of politics used in this chapter, and the approach to its analysis, it is not common to find illustrative books within the discipline of Politics as such. One is more likely to find good examples of this *kind* of approach in books by authors working in a variety of disciplines who more or less clearly share the approach adopted here. These may be found both in and outside the social and historical sciences. They are usually studies which in their own right are fascinating, too, in addition to their value for present purposes in illustrating the approach of this chapter. I list some titles which may not be immediately familiar to students in Politics. They are all well worth dipping into. All of them, in one way or another, illustrate the central thesis of this chapter that politics is fundamentally bound up with the use, production and distribution of resources, as are the problems which it generates.

A. L. Epstein, *Politics in an Urban African Community* (Manchester, 1958).

Stephen Gudeman, *The Demise of a Rural Economy: From Subsistence to Capitalism in a Latin American Village* (London, 1978).

Marvin Harris, *Cannibals and Kings* (Glasgow, 1978).

Marvin Harris, *Cultural Materialism: The struggle for a Science of Culture* (New York, 1980).

Adrian Leftwich, *Redefining Politics: People, Resources and Power* (London, 1983).

Barrington Moore, Jr, *Social Origins of Dictatorship and Democracy* (Boston, 1966).

W. W. Murdoch, *The Poverty of Nations* (Baltimore, 1980).

Daphne A. Roe, *A Plague of Corn: The Social History of Pellagra* (Ithaca, New York, 1973).

Amartya Sen, *Poverty and Famines* (Oxford, 1982).

Peter Townsend and Nick Davidson (eds), *Inequalities in Health* (Harmondsworth, 1982).

Richard G. Wilkinson, *Poverty and Progress* (London, 1973).

Bryan R. Wilson, *Magic and the Millennium* (London, 1973).

Godfrey and Monica Wilson, *The Analysis of Social Change* (Cambridge, 1954).

Donald Worster, *Dust Bowl: The Southern Plains in the 1930s* (New York and London, 1979).

Chapter 5: The levels of politics

On approaches to the study of politics, I recommend Preston King (ed.), *The Study of Politics: A Collection of Inaugural Lectures* (London, 1977); G. C. Moodie and G. Studdert-Kennedy, *Opinions, Publics and Pressure Groups* (London, 1970).

On power: Steven Lukes, *Power: A Radical View* (London, 1974); Niklas Luhman, *Trust and Power* (Chichester, 1979).

There is another rather odd book on 'bricks and mortar' in politics – Harold D. Lasswell and M. B. Fox, *The Signature of Power: Buildings, Communication and Policy* (New Brunswick, New Jersey, 1979).

On organization theory: Amitai Etzioni, *A Comparative Analysis of Complex Organizations* (Glencoe, Illinois, 1961); Charles Perrow, *Complex Organizations: A Critical Essay* (New York, 1972).

On symbol and ritual in politics: Murray Edelman, *The Symbolic Uses of Politics* (Urbana, Illinois, 1967), and *Politics as Symbolic Action* (Chicago, 1971); W. J. M. Mackenzie, *Political Identity* (Harmondsworth, 1978); and *Politics and Social Science* (Harmondsworth, 1967).

On the world crisis: Andre Gunder Frank, *Crisis: In the World Economy* (London, 1980); Nigel Harris, *Of Bread and Guns: The World Economy in Crisis* (Harmondsworth, 1983); Ian Roxborough, *Theories of Underdevelopment* (London, 1979).

Chapter 6: Political philosophy and politics

S. I. Benn and R. S. Peters, *Social Principles and the Democratic State* (London, 1959).

W. Connolly, *The Terms of Political Discourse* (Lexington, Mass., 1974).

R. E. Flathman (ed.), *Concepts in Social and Political Philosophy* (London, 1973).

D. Miller and L. Siedentop (eds), *The Nature of Political Theory* (Oxford, 1983).

M. Oakeshott, *On Human Conduct* (Oxford, 1975).

F. Oppenheim, *Political Concepts* (Oxford, 1981).

H. F. Pitkin, *Wittgenstein and Justice* (London, 1972).

J. Plamentaz, *Man and Society,* 2 vols. (London, 1963).

A. Quinton (ed.), *Political Philosophy* (Oxford, 1967).

D. D. Raphael, *Problems of Political Philosophy* (London, 1970).

J. Rawls, *A Theory of Justice* (Oxford, 1972).

A. Skillen, *Ruling Illusions* (Hassocks, Sussex, 1977).

T. D. Weldon, *The Vocabulary of Politics* (Harmondsworth, 1953).

Chapter 7: Marxism and politics

A. Callinicos, *The Revolutionary Ideas of Karl Marx* (London, 1983).

T. Cliff, *Lenin,* 4 vols. (London, 1975 – 79).

G. A. Cohen, *Karl Marx's Theory of History – A Defence* (Oxford, 1978).

H. Draper, *Karl Marx's Theory of Revolution,* 2 vols. (London, 1977, 1978).

A. Gilbert, *Marx's Politics* (Oxford, 1981).

A. Gramsci, *Selections from the Prison Notebooks* (London, 1971).

B. Jessop, *The Capitalist State* (Oxford, 1982).

V. I. Lenin, *Selected Works* (Moscow, 1970).

R. Luxemburg, *Selected Political Writings* (London, 1972).

K. Marx and F. Engels, *Selected Works* (Moscow, 1968).

R. Miliband, *The State in Capitalist Society* (London, 1969).

J. Molyneux, *Marxism and the Party* (London, 1978).

N. Poulantzas, *Political Power and Social Class* (London, 1973).

N. Poulantzas, *State, Power, Socialism* (London, 1978).

L. Trotsky, *The Struggle against Fascism in Germany* (New York, 1971).

Chapter 8: A discipline of Politics?

We see no point here in suggesting further reading on this topic. It will be more useful for readers to pursue some of the questions and arguments which have been raised in this chapter, and to apply them to their own studies and departments. Consider the following questions.

Around which conception – or conceptions – of politics is teaching in your department organized? Can a dominant one be identified? Which issues, approaches and perspectives predominate, and which are marginalized or excluded – and why?

What are the main components of your degree, how have these evolved and what is their rationale? How, if at all, are they related to one another? Is the emphasis on the learning of 'subjects' or on the development of related analytical skills for tackling political problems?

Are you convinced by the relative weighting and relevance of the component parts? Do they engage with serious historical or contemporary problems in politics and, if so, which ones? If not, why not, and what justification is given for this?

Is there room for innovation and change in the curriculum and methods of teaching? What are the opportunities for doing this and what are the constraints? Has there, in fact, been much discussion in your department about the nature and definition of politics and the appropriate role and scope for a discipline of Politics?

The kinds of issues raised here in relation to the politics of Politics can be applied to the organization of political life in any group, institution or society. How politics is shaped and constrained is open to question, always. And a vital politics, just as a vital Politics department, depends crucially on the constant pursuit of such questions.

Notes on Contributors

Alex Callinicos studied and taught at the University of Oxford. He is currently a lecturer in Politics in the University of York. He writes widely on political affairs and Marxism. He has published *Althusser's Marxism* (London, 1976); *Southern Africa after Soweto*, with John Rogers (London, 1977); *Southern Africa after Zimbabwe* (London, 1981); *Is there a Future for Marxism?* (London, 1982); *Marxism and Philosophy* (Oxford, 1983); and *The Revolutionary Ideas of Karl Marx* (London, 1983).

Andrew Dunsire is Professor and Head of the Department of Politics in the University of York. In the academic year 1983/84 he was visiting professor in the National University of Singapore. He has published widely in the field of public administration. His books include *Administration: The Word and the Science* (London, 1973); *Implementation in a Bureaucracy* (London, 1978); *Control in a Bureaucracy* (London, 1978); and *Bureaumetrics: The Quantitative Comparison of British Central Government Agencies,* with Christopher Hood (Farnborough, Gower, 1981).

David Held studied at the University of Manchester and at the Massachusetts Institute of Technology. He has held the University of Wales Fellowship, and thereafter taught in the department of Politics in the University of York. He is currently a lecturer in Social Science at the Open University. He has published in the fields of political theory and political sociology, and his books include *Introduction to Critical Theory: Horkheimer to Habermas* (London, 1980); *Habermas: Critical Debates*, edited with John B. Thompson (London, 1982); and *Classes, Power and Conflict: Classical and Contemporary Debates,* edited with Anthony Giddens (London, 1982).

John Horton studied at the University of Wales (Swansea) and is a lecturer in Politics in the University of York. His research interests are in the fields of political philosophy, the philosophy of the social sciences, and literature and politics. He is working on a book on Political Obligation.

Adrian Leftwich studied at the Universities of Cape Town and York. He has taught at both of them as well as at the Universities of Lancaster and Reading. He is currently a lecturer in Politics in the University of York. He has published articles in the field of university teaching methods. His books are *South Africa: Economic Growth and Political Change,* which he edited (London, 1974); .and *Redefining Politics: People, Resources and Power* (London, 1983).

Graeme C. Moodie is Professor of Politics in the University of York, where he established the department of Politics. His practical experience of politics includes having contested a seat at the British general election of 1959; fifteen years as head of the Politics department; seven years as head of one of the colleges at York, and three as deputy Vice-chancellor. He has published widely in the field of British government and politics, and also on university government. His books are *Some Problems of the Constitution,* with G. Marshall (London, 4th edn, 1967); *The Government of Great Britain* (London, 1964 and subsequent edns); *Opinions, Publics and Pressure Groups,* with Gerald Studdert-Kennedy (London, 1970); and *Power and Authority in British Universities,* with R. Eustace (London, 1974).

Peter P. Nicholson studied at the University of Exeter and lectured àt the University of Wales (Swansea). He is currently Senior Lecturer in Politics in the University of York. He has published many articles on political philosophy and on the history of political thought. He is completing a book on the political ideas of the British Idealists.

Albert Weale studied at the University of Cambridge, and thereafter undertook research and teaching as the Sir James Knott Fellow in the Department of Politics in the University of Newcastle-upon-Tyne. He has also taught at the Universtiy of Dar-es-Salaam in Tanzania, and is currently a lecturer in the Department of Politics in the University of York. He is closely associated with the Social Policy Research Unit at the University of York and is Assistant Director of the university's Institute for Research in the Social Sciences (IRISS). He has published widely in fields of political theory and social policy, and his books are *Equality and Social Policy* (London, 1978), and *Political Theory and Social Policy* (London, 1983).

Index

320
W555
194160

MR

AUTHOR

What is politics?

TITLE

DATE DUE	BORROWER'S NAME
MR 3 '87	
SE 2 '87	FE2 '87 RESERVE Eyrich 207

What is politics?   194160